TEACHER'S PET PUBLICATIONS

LITPLAN TEACHER PACK
for
Across Five Aprils
based on the book by
Irene Hunt

Written by
Mary B. Collins

© 1994 Teacher's Pet Publications
All Rights Reserved

This **LitPlan** for Irene Hunt's
Across Five Aprils
has been brought to you by Teacher's Pet Publications, Inc.

Copyright Teacher's Pet Publications 1994

Only the student materials in this unit plan
(such as worksheets, study questions, assignment sheets, and tests)
may be reproduced multiple times for use in the purchaser's classroom.

For any additional copyright questions,
contact Teacher's Pet Publications.

www.tpet.com

TABLE OF CONTENTS - *Across Five Aprils*

Introduction	5
Unit Objectives	7
Reading Assignment Sheet	8
Unit Outline	9
Study Questions (Short Answer)	13
Quiz/Study Questions (Multiple Choice)	25
Pre-reading Vocabulary Worksheets	49
Lesson One (Introductory Lesson)	65
Oral Reading Evaluation Form	73
Writing Assignment 1	70
Writing Assignment 2	75
Writing Assignment 3	87
Writing Evaluation Form	74
Vocabulary Review Activities	81
Extra Writing Assignments/Discussion ?s	79
Unit Review Activities	89
Unit Tests	93
Unit Resource Materials	127
Vocabulary Resource Materials	141

A FEW NOTES ABOUT THE AUTHOR
Irene Hunt

Irene Hunt was born May 18, 1907 in Newton, Illinois. In 1939 she received her A.B. degree from the University of Illinois, and in 1946 she received her M.A. degree from the University of Minnesota.

Ms. Hunt spent most of her career as a teacher: 1930-1945 in Oak Park, Illinois public schools, 1946-1950 at the University of South Dakota, and 1950-1965 in Cicero, Illinois public schools.

Across Five Aprils (1964) was Irene Hunt's first novel, for which she won the Charles W. Follett Award, the American Notable Book Award, and was the sole runner-up for the Newbery Medal. About *Across Five Aprils* Ms. Hunt said, "I didn't plan my first book for a certain age group. I don't want to aim at a special age of reader. I write when I have something to say, and I hope to say it as well and as gracefully as I can."

In 1966, *Up a Road Slowly,* a Newbery Medal winner, was published, followed by *Trail of Apple Blossoms* in 1968 and *No Promises in the Wind* in 1970.

INTRODUCTION

This unit has been designed to develop students' reading, writing, thinking, and language skills through exercises and activities related to *Across Five Aprils* by Irene Hunt. It includes eighteen lessons, supported by extra resource materials.

The **introductory lesson** introduces students to some background to the novel through a discussion with a guest speaker. Following the introductory activity, students are given a transition to explain how the activity relates to the book they are about to read. Following the transition, students are given the materials they will be using during the unit. At the end of the lesson, students begin the pre-reading work for the first reading assignment.

The **reading assignments** are approximately thirty pages each; some are a little shorter while others are a little longer. Students have approximately 15 minutes of pre-reading work to do prior to each reading assignment. This pre-reading work involves reviewing the study questions for the assignment and doing some vocabulary work for 8 to 10 vocabulary words they will encounter in their reading.

The **study guide questions** are fact-based questions; students can find the answers to these questions right in the text. These questions come in two formats: short answer or multiple choice. The best use of these materials is probably to use the short answer version of the questions as study guides for students (since answers will be more complete), and to use the multiple choice version for occasional quizzes. If your school has the appropriate machinery, it might be a good idea to make transparencies of your answer keys for the overhead projector.

The **vocabulary work** is intended to enrich students' vocabularies as well as to aid in the students' understanding of the book. Prior to each reading assignment, students will complete a two-part worksheet for approximately 8 to 10 vocabulary words in the upcoming reading assignment. Part I focuses on students' use of general knowledge and contextual clues by giving the sentence in which the word appears in the text. Students are then to write down what they think the words mean based on the words' usage. Part II nails down the definitions of the words by giving students dictionary definitions of the words and having students match the words to the correct definitions based on the words' contextual usage. Students should then have an understanding of the words when they meet them in the text.

After each reading assignment, students will go back and formulate answers for the study guide questions. Discussion of these questions serves as a **review** of the most important events and ideas presented in the reading assignments.

There is a **vocabulary review** lesson which pulls together all of the fragmented vocabulary lists for the reading assignments and gives students a review of all of the words they have studied.

A lesson is devoted to the **extra discussion questions/writing assignments**. These questions focus on interpretation, critical analysis and personal response, employing a variety of thinking skills and adding to the students' understanding of the novel.

There is a **group activity** in which students work in small groups to gather and present information about the people and places mentioned in the book.

There are three **writing assignments** in this unit, each with the purpose of informing, persuading, or having students express personal opinions. The first assignment is to inform: students write a short informative composition about the topic they have researched. This doubles as a preparation for the one-minute oral presentation students must give about their topics. The second assignment is to express personal opinions: students write letters to elected officials asking questions or expressing personal views about topics of the students' choice. The third assignment is to persuade: students write a letter to the man who said to Jethro, "Be glad you're a boy, young feller, and don't hev to pester yoreself with all these troubles that men be sufferin' through these days" persuading him that his statement was untrue.

In addition, there is a **nonfiction reading assignment**. Students are required to read a piece of nonfiction related in some way to *Across Five Aprils*. After reading their nonfiction pieces, students will fill out a worksheet on which they answer questions regarding facts, interpretation, criticism, and personal opinions.

The **review lesson** pulls together all of the aspects of the unit. The teacher is given four or five choices of activities or games to use which all serve the same basic function of reviewing all of the information presented in the unit.

The **unit test** comes in two formats: multiple choice or short answer. As a convenience, two different tests for each format have been included. There is also an advanced short answer test for students who need more of a challenge.

There are additional **support materials** included with this unit. The **extra activities section** includes suggestions for an in-class library, crossword and word search puzzles related to the novel, and extra vocabulary worksheets. There is a list of **bulletin board ideas** which gives the teacher suggestions for bulletin boards to go along with this unit. In addition, there is a list of **extra class activities** the teacher could choose from to enhance the unit or as a substitution for an exercise the teacher might feel is inappropriate for his/her class. **Answer keys** are located directly after the **reproducible student materials** throughout the unit. The student materials may be reproduced for use in the teacher's classroom without infringement of copyrights. No other portion of this unit may be reproduced without the written consent of Teacher's Pet Publications, Inc.

UNIT OBJECTIVES - *Across Five Aprils*

1. Through reading *Across Five Aprils* students will better understand the American Civil War.

2. Students will demonstrate their understanding of the text on four levels: factual, interpretive, critical, and personal.

3. Students will discuss family relationships, the theme of coming of age, the importance of education, the difficulties of war, and the relevance of the story to life today.

4. Students will be given the opportunity to practice reading aloud and silently to improve their skills in each area.

5. Students will answer questions to demonstrate their knowledge and understanding of the main events and characters in *Across Five Aprils* as they relate to the author's theme development.

6. Students will enrich their vocabularies and improve their understanding of the novel through the vocabulary lessons prepared for use in conjunction with the novel.

7. The writing assignments in this unit are geared to several purposes:
    a. To have students demonstrate their abilities to inform, to persuade, or to express their own personal ideas
        NOTE: Students will demonstrate ability to write effectively to <u>inform</u> by developing and organizing facts to convey information. Students will demonstrate the ability to write effectively to <u>persuade</u> by selecting and organizing relevant information, establishing an argumentative purpose, and by designing an appropriate strategy for an identified audience. Students will demonstrate the ability to write effectively to <u>express personal ideas</u> by selecting a form and its appropriate elements.
    b. To check the students' reading comprehension
    c. To make students think about the ideas presented by the novel
    d. To encourage logical thinking
    e. To provide an opportunity to practice good grammar and improve students' use of the English language.

8. Students will read aloud, report, and participate in large and small group discussions to improve their public speaking and personal interaction skills.

READING ASSIGNMENT SHEET - *Across Five Aprils*

Date Assigned	Chapters Assigned	Completion Date
	1-2	
	3-4	
	5	
	6-7	
	8-9	
	10-12	

UNIT OUTLINE - *Across Five Aprils*

1	2	3	4	5
Introduction PV 1-2	Library	Study ?s 1-2 Writing Assignment #1 PV 3-4	Reports Read 3-4	Study ?s 3-4 Reports PV 5
6 Read 5 PVR 6-7	**7** Writing Assignment #2	**8** Study ?s 5-7 PVR 8-9	**9** Study ?s 8-9 Grammar Worksheet PV 10-12	**10** Read 10-12
11 Study ?s 10-12 Extra ?s	**12** Extra ?s	**13** Vocabulary	**14** Writing Assignment #3	**15** Newspaper
16 Newspaper	**17** Review	**18** Test		

Key: P = Preview Study Questions V = Prereading Vocabulary Worksheet R = Read

STUDY GUIDE QUESTIONS

SHORT ANSWER STUDY GUIDE QUESTIONS - *Across Five Aprils*

Chapter 1
1. Describe Ellen.
2. Identify Jethro.
3. What kinds of things were troubling the adult world on that April morning?
4. Identify Jenny.
5. Who is Shadrach Yale?
6. How did Tom and Eb feel about the prospects of war?
7. What had happened to Jethro's sister, Mary?
8. To whom did Jethro compare his father? Why?
9. Who was Nancy?
10. Identify Bill.
11. Identify Wilse Graham.

Chapter 2
1. Why was Ellen particularly happy to see Cousin Wilse?
2. How did Wilse feel about slavery and the possibility of war?
3. How did Jethro's feelings towards war change after listening to the conversation among the men?
4. What news did Shadrach bring?

Chapter 3
1. What happened on Saturday and Sunday nights in southern Illinois?
2. What effect did the Confederate victories at Bull Run and Ball's Bluff have on the Northerners?
3. Why was the battle of Wilson's Creek a scare to the Creightons?
4. How did Bill comfort Jethro in the middle of the night?
5. What about Pa and John angered Bill?
6. What did Jethro do at Walnut Hill when he was little?
7. Why was Bill's face bruised?
8. Why did Bill have to leave?

Chapter 4
1. At what point did the Union begin to win more battles?
2. Why did Ellen give the letter to Jethro?
3. What did Tom's letter say?
4. Why was Jenny upset about the war?
5. Why did Jethro go to Shad's house?
6. How did Shad make Jethro understand the war?
7. What were Jethro's thoughts as he fell to sleep?

Across Five Aprils Short Answer Study Guide Page 2

Chapter 5
1. Why was Ellen upset by her headaches?
2. When Jethro went to borrow the coffee from Nancy, what surprised him?
3. Why was Jethro so proud that he was going to town?
4. Who did Jethro meet on the road, and what did the man want?
5. What did Sam Gardiner give Jethro? Why?
6. What trouble did Jethro have in Newton?
7. Why did Mr. Milton want Jethro to leave early?
8. What happened after Jethro passed the Burdow place?
9. What happened to Jethro and Dave Burdow by the bridge?
10. Why was Roscoe muttering angrily at his gate?
11. What did Jethro leave out of his original story to the family? Why?

Chapter 6
1. What was wrong with Matt?
2. Why did Ellen think she was a soft mother?
3. Why did Jethro say he had left childhood behind him in that March of 1862?
4. Why did Jenny think that Jethro and Shad were alike?
5. Why was Jethro angry with Jenny?
6. How did Jenny try to comfort Jethro about the letter?
7. What warning did the men on horseback bring in the middle of the night?
8. What was the feeling of the community towards the Creightons?
9. What happened to the Creightons' barn?

Chapter 7
1. How did the community show support for Matt Creighton that spring?
2. What news did Dan Lawrence bring?
3. What kind of letter did Ross Milton put into his paper?
4. Why did Jenny stop making plans?
5. How did Guy Wortman get what was coming to him?

Chapter 8
1. Why did Jethro hate to think of Shiloh?
2. Why was the Union army demoralized in 1862?
3. What did the men think of General McClellan?
4. What happened to McClellan?
5. Who was Ambrose Burnside?
6. Although Stones River had been a victory, what did John write to Nancy about it?

Across Five Aprils Short Answer Study Guide Page 3

Chapter 9
1. What was going on at Point Prospect?
2. Why did the Federal Registrars visit the Creightons' farm?
3. What was Jenny's reaction to the Registrars?
4. Who was the "wild turkey"?
5. How did Eb feel about deserting?
6. How did Jethro feel about harboring Eb?
7. What did Jenny think was bothering Jethro?
8. What did Jethro do to solve his problem with Eb?
9. From whom did Jethro get an important letter, and what did it say?

Chapter 10
1. Identify Joe Hooker.
2. What did Shad's letter to Jenny say?
3. What did Eb do when he rejoined the army?
4. What were people's feelings about the battle at Gettysburg?
5. Why did Jenny go to Washington?
6. Was Jenny's trip to Washington worthwhile?

Chapter 11
1. What happened at Chickamauga?
2. What was John upset about in his letter?
3. What comforted John?
4. What did Shad think of General Grant?
5. What did Shad think of McClellan's nomination for President?
6. When did the North begin to rejoice?
7. Why was Lincoln re-elected?
8. What message did Bill send?

Chapter 12
1. What was Sherman's gift to Lincoln?
2. What did Ed Turner think of the soldiers' looting?
3. What were Ross Milton's thoughts about peace?
4. What were Ross Milton's thoughts about the thirteenth amendment?
5. What happened in the second week of April?
6. What bad news did Nancy bring to Jethro?
7. How did Jethro feel about Lincoln's death?
8. Who was the gaunt soldier who found Jethro in the field?
9. What was Shad's plan for Jethro?

ANSWER KEY: SHORT ANSWER STUDY GUIDE QUESTIONS - *Across Five Aprils*

Chapter 1

1. Describe Ellen.
    Ellen was a hard-working woman who did not miss or value her long-lost beauty. She had borne twelve children and had survived through thirty years of sickness and poverty.

2. Identify Jethro.
    Jethro is Ellen's nine year-old son, the youngest of twelve children. Being the youngest, because he had survived through the illness which had claimed the lives of several of his siblings, and because he showed some special talents, he was indulged more than the other children were.

3. What kinds of things were troubling the adult world on that April morning?
    The adults were troubled by chinch bugs, grasshoppers, drought, elections, slavery, secession, and talk of war.

4. Identify Jenny.
    Jenny is Ellen's fourteen-year-old daughter who helps with the cooking and other household work. She is in love with Shadrach Yale.

5. Who is Shadrach Yale?
    He is the school teacher. He is very close to the Creighton family, is in love with Jenny, and sees great promise in Jethro.

6. How did Tom and Eb feel about the prospects of war?
    They thought it was exciting; they were looking forward to getting the war underway and joining up in the military to fight for the South.

7. What had happened to Jethro's sister, Mary?
    She had been at a dance when some uninvited guests arrived and the party became dangerous. She and her friend left, but they were followed by Travis Burdow. Rob had tried to get to a safe place, but Travis Burdow had fired a shot and scared the horses. The wagon flipped over, killing Mary.

8. To whom did Jethro compare his father? Why?
    He compared his father to Abe Lincoln because neither of them wanted bloodshed. His father argued against hanging Travis Burdow and Mr. Lincoln wouldn't call for war.

9. Who was Nancy?
    Nancy was Jethro's sister-in-law. She married his brother, John. She was very quiet because her own relatives had treated her so badly. Her quiet ways made it difficult for her to become close to John's family.

10. Identify Bill.

Bill was Jethro's favorite brother. He was considered peculiar by most people because he liked to read and cared very little for "masculine" things like wrestling. He was a strong worker, though, and everyone liked him. Bill and John were very close brothers.

11. Identify Wilse Graham.

Wilse Graham was Ellen's nephew from Kentucky. During his short visit he got into an argument with the family about the upcoming war. He brought to the surface everyone's true feelings about the North and the South.

Chapter 2

1. Why was Ellen particularly happy to see Cousin Wilse?

He brought news of her family in Kentucky.

2. How did Wilse feel about slavery and the possibility of war?

He felt that the north was wrong. He believed that slavery was tolerable and that the north had become arrogant toward the south.

3. How did Jethro's feelings towards war change after listening to the conversation among the men?

He became troubled by war. Although the prospect of glorious war once excited his imagination, he began to fear what war would bring.

4. What news did Shadrach bring?

He brought news that the Confederates had fired on Fort Sumter. The war had begun even though Congress had not officially declared it.

Chapter 3

1. What happened on Saturday and Sunday nights in southern Illinois?

The weekend evenings became like the Fourth of July with brass bands, speakers, and picnics.

2. What effect did the Confederate victories at Bull Run and Ball's Bluff have on the Northerners?

They began to understand that a victory for the North would not come as easily as they had thought it would.

3. Why was the battle of Wilson's Creek a scare to the Creightons?

The battle had been close to home, and the Union had lost.

4. How did Bill comfort Jethro in the middle of the night?

Bill told Jethro that everyone was scared at times and that being scared was nothing to be ashamed of.

5. What about Pa and John angered Bill?
   He was angered because they were so sure of their beliefs.

6. What did Jethro do at Walnut Hill when he was little?
   He pretended that his brothers were still alive and were his playmates.

7. Why was Bill's face bruised?
   He and John had been fighting about their differences of opinion regarding the war.

8. Why did Bill have to leave?
   He wasn't so sure that his father and brothers were right in supporting the North. He thought that possibly the South had the better cause. He left home to avoid constant arguments and fights in the family, to become more sure of his own feelings, and, eventually, to fight for the South.

<u>Chapter 4</u>

1. At what point did the Union begin to win more battles?
   The Union began to win after the fall of Fort Henry in Tennessee.

2. Why did Ellen give the letter to Jethro?
   She could not read.

3. What did Tom's letter say?
   He let everyone know that he and Eb were safe and told Jethro that being a soldier wasn't so great.

4. Why was Jenny upset about the war?
   Shad would be going off to war before her father would allow her to marry him.

5. Why did Jethro go to Shad's house?
   He went to let him read Tom's letter and to give his mother some time alone.

6. How did Shad make Jethro understand the war?
   He drew a sketch of the position of the troops to help Jethro understand why the war would not be over soon.

7. What were Jethro's thoughts as he fell to sleep?
   He thought about the war, the cold, President Lincoln, Jenny and Shad, and how Tom had done a fine thing.

Chapter 5

1. Why was Ellen upset by her headaches?
    She hated to admit that she was dependent on coffee, which was becoming extremely expensive during the war time.

2. When Jethro went to borrow the coffee from Nancy, what surprised him?
    He had never heard her talk so much at one time.

3. Why was Jethro so proud that he was going to town?
    It was the first time that his father had let him go to town by himself. He was being trusted with the horse, wagon, money, and goods. It was a step towards his manhood.

4. Who did Jethro meet on the road, and what did the man want?
    Jethro met Jake Roscoe. He talked about the battle at Pea Ridge and asked Jethro to get a newspaper for him. He couldn't read, but he could recognize his grandson's name if it were in the paper.

5. What did Sam Gardiner give Jethro? Why?
    He gave Jethro a handful of gumdrops because he had seen Jethro's horrified look when he had put a gumdrop on an oil can to prevent it from spilling.

6. What trouble did Jethro have in Newton?
    Some men at the store harassed him because Bill had gone to fight with the Rebs.

7. Why did Mr. Milton want Jethro to leave early?
    He was afraid that the men who had given Jethro trouble at the store would cause him harm on his way home. He wanted Jethro to leave town before the men did so he would be safe.

8. What happened after Jethro passed the Burdow place?
    Dave Burdow jumped onto his wagon to ride with him for a while.

9. What happened to Jethro and Dave Burdow by the bridge?
    A man tried to attack them and scared the horses. Had Dave Burdow not been there to hold the team steady, Jethro may have been killed by an overturned wagon.

10. Why was Roscoe muttering angrily at his gate?
    Jethro would (could) not talk to him or introduce the other man in the wagon.

11. What did Jethro leave out of his original story to the family? Why?
    He left out the parts about the threats in the store, the incident with Dave Burdow, and the incident at the bridge because he thought his family would worry too much if they knew the truth.

Chapter 6

1. What was wrong with Matt?
    He was so worried that he had a stroke.

2. Why did Ellen think she was a soft mother?
    She let Jethro sleep in the morning after his trip to Newton.

3. Why did Jethro say he had left childhood behind him in that March of 1862?
    He had learned about war and was faced with being the man of the house since the older men were gone and his father was disabled.

4. Why did Jenny think that Jethro and Shad were alike?
    She thought both of them were too somber and needed a foolish girl to cheer them up.

5. Why was Jethro angry with Jenny?
    She would not let him read the letter from Shad.

6. How did Jenny try to comfort Jethro about the letter?
    She offered to let him read it alone, saying that she just didn't want to upset their father.

7. What warning did the men on horseback bring in the middle of the night?
    They threw a bundle of switches with a note attached saying, "Theres trubel fer fokes that stands up fer there reb lovin sons."

8. What was the feeling of the community towards the Creightons?
    Most of the people saw the Creightons as a good family with one wayward son. Most of them supported Matt Creighton. Some, however, were infuriated with them because they would not speak badly of Bill.

9. What happened to the Creightons' barn?
    Some people who were angry about Bill set fire to their barn.

Chapter 7

1. How did the community show support for Matt Creighton that spring?
    They cleaned the well and donated grain, hay, plows, and harnesses, and many men came to help out in the fields.

2. What news did Dan Lawrence bring?
    He brought the news of Tom's death.

3. What kind of a letter did Ross Milton put into his paper?
>He wrote a letter to the people who had been harassing the Creightons. In the letter he said that the Creightons had suffered enough by losing a son fighting for the Union, and he asked what sacrifices the night vandals had made for the Union.

4. Why did Jenny stop making plans?
>She was afraid that the plans would be for a time that would never happen; she was afraid that Shad would be killed in the war.

5. How did Guy Wortman get what was coming to him?
>He broke into Sam Gardiner's store to vandalize it one night when he thought Sam was out of town. Sam was in the store waiting for Guy, and he shot him in the backside. Everyone in town made fun of Guy Wortman for being shot in the butt, and everyone knew that he had been caught red-handed.

Chapter 8

1. Why did Jethro hate to think of Shiloh?
>He considered it to be an empty victory just like Pittsburgh Landing. They were victories for the Union, but they didn't seem to lead to an end of the war.

2. Why was the Union army demoralized in 1862?
>Criticism of the President poured in, faith in the leaders was very low, and desertions were widespread.

3. What did the men think of General McClellan?
>They thought he was a fool who would never fight to win the war for the North. They thought he was a braggart and a vain man.

4. What happened to McClellan?
>The President relieved him of his command.

5. Who was Ambrose Burnside?
>He was a Union general who sent thousands of Union soldiers to their deaths in the hills of Virginia.

6. Although Stones River had been a victory, what did John write to Nancy about it?
>He wrote that there were 13,000 casualties and that he hated war.

Chapter 9

1. What was going on at Point Prospect?
>Deserters were camping there, stealing food, and terrorizing the neighborhood.

2. Why did the Federal Registrars visit the Creightons' farm?
> They were looking for Eb. They knew that he had deserted the army and strongly suspected that he was making his way home.

3. What was Jenny's reaction to the Registrars?
> She was truly angry with them for even suspecting that Eb was there. She coolly told them to look everywhere and helped them search the farm, all the while making cool remarks to them. Jethro thought Jenny was grand when she was angry.

4. Who was the "wild turkey"?
> Eb was the "turkey" in the woods. He had used the turkey call so that no one would realize that he was in the woods.

5. How did Eb feel about deserting?
> He wished he hadn't done it, and he wished he could go back and fight with his unit again.

6. How did Jethro feel about harboring Eb?
> He had mixed feelings. He honored Tom for bravely facing a Confederate bullet and could see that it wasn't quite right for Eb to be sneaking out. However, he thought that Eb had been brave for two years and deserved some credit for that, and he thought of Eb as being sick and needing help.

7. What did Jenny think was bothering Jethro?
> She thought that Jethro had been smoking and had made himself sick with the smoke.

8. What did Jethro do to solve his problem with Eb?
> He wrote a letter to President Lincoln to ask for advice as to how to solve Eb's problem.

9. From whom did Jethro get an important letter, and what did it say?
> He got a letter from President Lincoln which said if Eb would go to a designated center by April first, he would be able to rejoin the army without punishment.

Chapter 10

1. Identify Joe Hooker.
> He was an arrogant general who created his own downfall at Chancellorsville.

2. What did Shad's letter to Jenny say?
> He told her that she should prepare for the probability of heartbreak.

3. What did Eb do when he rejoined the army?
    He was put to the task of digging ditches. He received the scorn of other soldiers who had not deserted, but he didn't mind because he was ashamed of his desertion and felt as though he deserved whatever scorn he received. He just decided to take his punishment and do the best he could for as long as need be.

4. What were people's feelings about the battle at Gettysburg?
    They were glad for the victory, but they almost couldn't believe that the Union had once again given up the opportunity of totally crushing Lee's army.

5. Why did Jenny go to Washington?
    Shad was there. He had been wounded and was in critical condition. Shad's aunt sent for her, Matt gave his permission for her to go, and Ross Milton escorted her.

6. Was Jenny's trip to Washington worthwhile?
    Yes, Shad got better and they were married.

Chapter 11

1. What happened at Chickamauga?
    Chickamauga was a devastating defeat for the North, but John managed to live through it.

2. What was John upset about in his letter?
    He was upset that his unit was treated like a third-rate unit, given the easy job, and teased by the other units.

3. What comforted John?
    He was comforted by the fact that his one last brother was close to his little boys.

4. What did Shad think of General Grant?
    He had confidence that this man would win the war for the North.

5. What did Shad think of McClellan's nomination for President?
    He was pleased to see McClellan nominated although he was still for Mr. Lincoln.

6. When did the North begin to rejoice?
    They began to rejoice when Sherman took Mobile and Alabama.

7. Why was Lincoln re-elected?
    The North was having success in the war, and the people saw no reason to give up the winning leader. Had the North still been doing poorly in the war, Lincoln may not have been re-elected.

8. What message did Bill send?
>He was a prisoner in a Union camp, and he sent word to his mother that he was not at Pittsburgh Landing; the bullet that killed Tom was not his.

Chapter 12

1. What was Sherman's gift to Lincoln?
>The city of Savannah was his gift.

2. What did Ed Turner think of the soldiers' looting?
>Since the whole North was cheering the soldiers' actions, he was afraid it would teach his son that looting and ruthlessness were good behavior. He was afraid his son would lose the morals he had been taught.

3. What were Ross Milton's thoughts about peace?
>He thought that peace would be hard to come by and that the scars from the war would be a long time in healing.

4. What were Ross Milton's thoughts about the thirteenth amendment?
>He was for the amendment, but he was afraid that the North would not know what to do with the freed slaves. He suspected that it would be decades before the reality of the dream of the thirteenth amendment would be realized.

5. What happened in the second week of April?
>The South surrendered to the North at Appomattox Court House in Virginia.

6. What bad news did Nancy bring to Jethro?
>She told him that President Lincoln had been assassinated.

7. How did Jethro feel about Lincoln's death?
>He thought it was terribly unfair that Lincoln died. He was the country's hope for peace, and he was gone. Jethro took Lincoln's death personally; he had wanted to shake Mr. Lincoln's hand, to see the great man who had taken the time to write back such heartfelt words to him.

8. Who was the gaunt soldier who found Jethro in the field?
>Shad had come home.

9. What was Shad's plan for Jethro?
>He planned that Jethro would come to live with him and Jenny while going to school.

MULTIPLE CHOICE STUDY GUIDE/QUIZ QUESTIONS - *Across Five Aprils*

Chapter 1

1. Which of the following does not describe Ellen?
    - A. She had kept her youthful beauty.
    - B. She was a hard-working woman.
    - C. She had borne twelve children.
    - D. She had survived through thirty years of sickness and poverty.

2. Who is Jethro?
    - A. He is the son of Ellen's sister. When her sister died in childbirth, Ellen adopted Jethro to raise as her own.
    - B. He is the middle child of Ellen's many children.
    - C. He is Ellen's nine year old, the youngest of her children.
    - D. He is the second oldest son. He was sick as a youngster and so is not able to do the heavy work the others do. Ellen pampers him, much to the dislike of the others.

3. Which of the following was not troubling the adult world on that April morning?
    - A. Cinchbugs and grasshoppers
    - B. Drought
    - C. Secession and talk of war
    - D. Inflation

4. Who is Jenny?
    - A. She is a young girl from the town who comes every day to help Ellen.
    - B. She is Ellen's fourteen-year-old daughter.
    - C. She is the schoolteacher's sister, who has come from the East to be his assistant.
    - D. She is Eb's niece, who lives with them.

5. Which of these does not describe Shadrach Yale?
    - A. He is the schoolteacher.
    - B. He is in love with Jenny.
    - C. He sees promise in Jethro.
    - D. He lives on the land owned by the Burdow family.

6. How did Tom and Eb feel about the prospects of war?
    - A. They were looking forward to fighting for the South.
    - B. They were looking forward to fighting for the North.
    - C. They both opposed the war and refused to fight.
    - D. They were undecided about which side they were going to support.

Across Five Aprils Multiple Choice Study Questions Page 2

7. What had happened to Jethro's sister, Mary?
   A. She had been walking along the train tracks and got her foot caught in a rail. She was not able to get out in time and was killed by an oncoming train.
   B. She got involved with a group of abolitionists who were traveling through town on their way North. She left her home and family to go with them.
   C. She was on her way home from a dance with a friend when someone fired a shot and scared their horses. The wagon flipped over and killed her.
   D. The schoolteacher had recognized her great intellect and had arranged for her to receive a scholarship from a prestigious girls' school in the East. She had left home a few months prior to the beginning of the story.

8. To whom did Jethro compare his father, and why?
   A. He compared his father to Thomas Jefferson because they were both from Virginia.
   B. He compared his father to Abraham Lincoln because neither wanted bloodshed.
   C. He compared his father to Benjamin Franklin because they were both great inventors.
   D. He compared his father to Moses because he believed in taking care of his people.

9. Which of the following does not describe Nancy?
   A. She is married to Jethro's brother, John.
   B. She is not close to the rest of her husband's family.
   C. She was treated badly by her own relatives.
   D. She is loud and argumentative.

10. This character is Jethro's favorite brother. He is considered peculiar by most people and would rather read than do "masculine "things. He was a strong worker and well-liked. Who is this?
    A. Bill
    B. John
    C. Eb
    D. Ross

11. True or False: Wilse Graham is Ellen's nephew from Kentucky. While visiting, he brought everyone's true feelings about the North and South to the surface.
    A. True
    B. False

Across Five Aprils Multiple Choice Study Questions Page 3

Chapter 2

12. Why was Ellen happy to see Wilse?
    A. He brought molasses and other supplies that she couldn't get locally.
    B. He brought news of her family in another state.
    C. He knew how to read and was able to read the newspaper to them.
    D. He represented the city and the finer things in life.

13. How did Wilse feel about the possibility of war?
    A. He felt the South was wrong and should surrender to the North.
    B. He felt that the war would devastate the entire country and should be avoided at all costs.
    C. He was primarily interested in profit and planned to sell goods to both sides. He didn't care who won.
    D. He thought the North was arrogant and that slavery was tolerable.

14. How did Jethro's feelings towards war change after listening to the conversation among the men?
    A. He became troubled and feared what war would bring.
    B. He was excited at the glorious prospects of fighting.
    C. He became sad at the prospect of so many deaths.
    D. He wished he lived in the North.

15. True or False: Shadrach brought the news that Congress had officially declared war
    A. True
    B. False

Across Five Aprils Multiple Choice Study Questions Page 4

Chapter 3

16. What happened on Saturday and Sunday nights in southern Illinois?
    A. There were barn dances and hoe-downs.
    B. The people gathered at one farmhouse to listen to someone who could read the newspaper to them and talk about current events.
    C. They had brass bands, speakers, and picnics.
    D. These evenings were reserved for prayer meetings and revivals.

17. True or False: The Confederate victories at Bull Run and Ball's Bluff inspired the Northern army. They thought victory was only a few weeks away
    A. True
    B. False

18. True or False: The battle of Wilson's Creek was a scare to the Creightons because the Union had lost and the battle was close to home
    A. True
    B. False

19. How did Bill comfort Jethro in the middle of the night?
    A. Bill told Jethro that everyone was scared at times and it was nothing to be afraid of.
    B. Bill gave Jethro a cup of warm milk and a piece of cornbread.
    C. Bill sang patriotic songs to Jethro.
    D. Bill read Jethro's favorite parts of the Bible to him.

20. What about Pa and John angered Bill?
    A. They never listened to anyone else.
    B. They were not very kind to their women and children.
    C. They were so sure of their beliefs.
    D. They were all talk and no action.

21. What did Jethro do at Walnut Hill when he was little?
    A. He killed and skinned a rabbit.
    B. He listened in on his parents having an argument.
    C. He stole his father's rifle and practiced shooting.
    D. He pretended that his brothers were still alive and were his playmates.

22. Why was Bill's face bruised?
    A. He fell off his horse, got his foot caught in the stirrup, and was dragged several feet.
    B. He had a fight with John about their differences of opinion regarding the war.
    C. He had been milking the cow and had been accidentally kicked.
    D. He had talked back to his mother, and his father had slapped him.

Across Five Aprils Multiple Choice Study Questions Page 5

23. True or False: Bill left home to become more sure of his own feelings and to avoid constant arguments and to eventually fight for the South
    A. True
    B. False

Across Five Aprils Multiple Choice Study Questions Page 6

<u>Chapter 4</u>

24. At what point did the Union begin to win more battles?
    A. It was at Fort Ticonderoga.
    B. It was at Gettysburg.
    C. It was at Fort Henry.
    D. It was at Fort Sumter.

25. What did Ellen do with the letter?
    A. She gave it to Jethro because she could not read.
    B. She saved it for her husband to read first.
    C. She put it on top of the cabinet and forgot about it.
    D. She went into her room and read it privately first, then shared it.

26. What did Tom's letter say?
    A. He was safe, but Eb had been injured.
    B. Conditions were terrible, but morale was great.
    C. He and his brother were pleased with their decisions.
    D. Being a soldier wasn't so great, but they were both safe.

27. Why was Jenny upset about the war?
    A. She couldn't get any fabric to make new dresses or quilts.
    B. Shad would be going off to war before her father would allow her to marry him.
    C. She wanted to fight, but women were not permitted to join the service.
    D. She was afraid it would come to their area and they would all be killed.

28. Why did Jethro go to Shad's house?
    A. He wanted to talk to Shad about "manly things."
    B. He needed help on a homework assignment.
    C. He wanted to show Shad Tom's letter and leave his mother alone for a while.
    D. Shad let Jethro smoke when they were alone together.

29. How did Shad make Jethro understand the war?
    A. He read articles from the newspaper aloud to Jethro.
    B. He dramatized a battle.
    C. He drew a sketch of the positions of the troops.
    D. He sang a song he had written for the students.

Across Five Aprils Multiple Choice Study Questions Page 7

30. Which was not one of Jethro's thoughts as he fell asleep?
- A. He thought about his father being too old to fight.
- B. He thought about the cold.
- C. He thought about President Lincoln.
- D. He thought about how Tom had done a fine thing.

Across Five Aprils Multiple Choice Study Questions Page 8

Chapter 5

31. Why was Ellen upset?
    A. The corn crop was near ruin due to the drought.
    B. She hated to admit that she was dependent on coffee, which was becoming extremely expensive.
    C. She wanted to spend more time with her grandchildren but was always busy working.
    D. She realized that Jethro was growing up and might have to fight in the war if it didn't end soon.

32. When Jethro went on his errand to Nancy's house, what surprised him?
    A. She wasn't home.
    B. She was still asleep.
    C. She had hung a Union flag over the front porch railing.
    D. She was very talkative.

33. How did Jethro feel about going to town?
    A. He was scared but refused to show it.
    B. He didn't want to go but was doing it because his father told him to.
    C. He was proud and saw it as a step toward manhood.
    D. He was angry because he had to miss school to go.

34. Who did Jethro meet, and what did he want?
    A. He met the preacher, who wanted a ride to town.
    B. He met Jake Roscoe, who wanted a newspaper.
    C. He met Nancy, who wanted ribbons and flour from the store.
    D. He met Ross Milton, who wanted him to mail a letter.

35. True or False: Sam Gardiner gave Jethro a handful of gumdrops because he had seen Jethro's horrified look when he had put a gumdrop on an oil can to prevent it from spilling.
    A. True
    B. False

36. What trouble did Jethro have in Newton?
    A. He didn't know how to park the wagon.
    B. He got lost and couldn't find the store.
    C. Some men harassed him because Bill had gone to fight with the Rebs.
    D. He didn't have enough money to pay for everything he bought. The shopkeeper thought Jethro was trying to cheat him.

Across Five Aprils Multiple Choice Study Questions Page 9

37. What did Mr. Milton want Jethro to do?
    A. He wanted Jethro to spend the night with him and leave early the next morning.
    B. He wanted Jethro to leave early and avoid trouble on his way home.
    C. He offered to give Jethro a gun to use to protect himself.
    D. He wanted Jethro to go home by another route, one that was not familiar to Jethro.

38. What happened after Jethro passed the Burdow place?
    A. Dave Burdow jumped into his wagon to ride with him for a while.
    B. One of the horses got a stone in its hoof and Jethro had to walk.
    C. Jethro got tired and pulled his wagon onto the Burdow's land to take a nap.
    D. Jethro yelled a curse at the house and its inhabitants.

39. What happened by the bridge?
    A. The bridge collapsed.
    B. Jethro found a dead body with a Confederate flag draped over it.
    C. A snake scared the horse, and Jethro had to fight to keep control of them.
    D. Someone tried to attack the wagon and scare the horses. Dave Burdow saved Jethro by holding the team steady.

40. Why was Roscoe muttering angrily at his gate?
    A. A snake scared the horses and Jethro had to fight to keep control of them. Jethro was late and Roscoe had missed his nightly card game to wait for him.
    B. Jethro had forgotten to bring the newspaper.
    C. He had just heard news about another Confederate victory.
    D. Jethro would (could) not talk to him or introduce the other man in the wagon.

41. True or False: When retelling the day's events, Jethro left out the parts that he thought would worry his family too much
    A. True
    B. False

Across Five Aprils Multiple Choice Study Questions Page 10

Chapter 6

42. What was wrong with Matt?
    A. He was depressed.
    B. He had a stroke.
    C. He had an ulcer.
    D. He had appendicitis.

43. Why did Ellen think she was a soft mother?
    A. She let Jethro sleep in the morning after his trip.
    B. She fed her son breakfast in bed.
    C. She let Jethro stay up and talk with the adults.
    D. She let Jethro miss school because he didn't feel well.

44. What happened in March of 1862?
    A. Jethro inherited a large sum of money.
    B. Jethro went away to college.
    C. Jethro became the man of the house and left his childhood behind him.
    D. Jethro was old enough to enlist in the army.

45. Why did Jenny think that Jethro and Shad were alike?
    A. They both liked to read and read the same books
    B. They were born on the same day.
    C. They were both quite absent-minded.
    D. They were both somber and needed someone to cheer them up.

46. Why was Jethro angry with Jenny?
    A. She would not make his favorite pie.
    B. She would not let him read the letter from Shad.
    C. She had used his pen and paper without permission.
    D. She had made fun of his efforts to learn about the war.

47. How did Jenny try to comfort Jethro after their argument?
    A. She offered to do his chores for a week.
    B. She apologized.
    C. She said she had not wanted to upset their father, and then offered to do what she had originally refused to do.
    D. She cried and acted upset so he could feel like the man of the house.

Across Five Aprils Multiple Choice Study Questions Page 11

48. How did the Creightons hear the following warning: "Theres trubel fer fokes that stands up fer there reb lovin sons?"
    A. Some men on horseback threw a bundle of switches with a note attached.
    B. Someone painted the words on the side of their barn.
    C. A group of men shouted it under their window.
    D. Some of the townspeople took out an ad in the local paper.

49. True or False: The entire community was against the Creightons.
    A. True
    B. False

50. What happened to the Creightons' barn?
    A. It was set on fire.
    B. It was destroyed in a tornado.
    C. It was eaten by termites.
    D. It was taken over by a military troop and used to store supplies.

Across Five Aprils Multiple Choice Study Questions Page 12

<u>Chapter 7</u>

51. How did the community show support for Matt Creighton that spring?
    A. They paid his mortgage.
    B. The men took turns driving him to the doctor in the next town.
    C. They donated grain and equipment and worked his fields.
    D. They held a "Matt Creighton Appreciation Day" service at church.

52. What news did Dan Lawrence bring?
    A. Tom and Eb had both been captured.
    B. Tom had died.
    C. Eb had died.
    D. Eb had been captured by the enemy, but Tom was missing.

53. What kind of letter did Ross Milton put into his paper?
    A. He said the Creightons had suffered enough by the sacrifices their sons had made and asked the night vandals what they had done for the Union.
    B. He offered a substantial reward for any information about the identification of the vandals.
    C. He called for the town to unite and have a Union Support Day where they all made bandages and wrote letters to the soldiers.
    D. He prayed for a quick end to the war.

54. True or False: Jenny accelerated her wedding and other plans. She wanted to try to get everything in early, in case Shad was killed in the war.
    A. True
    B. False

55. What happened to Guy Wortman?
    A. He was drafted by the Confederate army.
    B. He was wounded in battle and was sent home a hero.
    C. He broke into Sam Gardiner's store, and Sam shot him in the backside.
    D. He had a religious conversion, confessed all of his past sins, and made retribution to everyone he had wronged.

Across Five Aprils Multiple Choice Study Questions Page 13

Chapter 8

56. What was Jethro's opinion of the battle of Shiloh?
    A. He thought the North was one step closer to winning.
    B. He thought it was an empty victory, that didn't seem to lead to an end to the war.
    C. He thought it was the most important battle of the war.
    D. He thought the South was one step closer to winning.

57. Which is not one of the reasons the Union army was demoralize in 1862?
    A. There was criticism of the President.
    B. The soldiers didn't have faith in their leaders.
    C. Desertions were widespread.
    D. There was a cholera epidemic among the troops.

58. What did the men think of General Mc Clellan?
    A. They thought he was a braggart and a fool who would never win the war.
    B. They thought he was marginal but was the best possible choice.
    C. They wholeheartedly supported him.
    D. Their opinions were split, which was also causing dissention among the troops.

59. What happened to McClellan?
    A. He was promoted to a White House staff position.
    B. He was relieved of his command.
    C. He had a heart attack and went on medical disability leave.
    D. He resigned and fled to Europe.

60. Who was Ambrose Burnside?
    A. He was a famous newspaper reporter who chronicled the war in great detail.
    B. He was the military strategic advisor to the President.
    C. He was a Union general who sent thousands of soldiers to their deaths in the hills of Virginia.
    D. He was a doctor who developed new treatments for treating wounded soldiers right on the battlefield.

61. What did John write to Nancy about the war?
    A. He said it was almost over.
    B. He said there were 13,000 casualties at the battle of Stones River and he hated the war.
    C. He said he was thinking about deserting.
    D. He admitted that the sound of gun and cannon fire scared him.

Across Five Aprils Multiple Choice Study Questions Page 14

Chapter 9

62. What was going on at Point Prospect?
    A. There was a prisoner of war camp.
    B. There was a field hospital that was treating wounded from both sides.
    C. A group of pacifists were organizing to march on Washington.
    D. Deserters were camping there, terrorizing the neighborhood.

63. Why did the Federal Registrars visit the Creightons' farm?
    A. They were looking for Eb, who had deserted.
    B. They were looking for more boys to enlist. Someone had told them that Jethro was old enough to go.
    C. They were looking for a place to set up a spying operation and wanted to use the Creighton farm.
    D. Matt Creighton owed back taxes, and they were there to collect.

64. What was Jenny's reaction to the Registrars?
    A. She was pleasant an helpful.
    B. She was cool and angry.
    C. She was afraid of them and hid.
    D. She flirted with one of the younger man.

65. How did Eb reveal himself to Jethro without being seen by anyone else?
    A. He dressed in a deer skin, complete with antlers.
    B. He used a secret code only he and Jethro knew to blaze a trail to his hideout.
    C. He gave wild turkey call.
    D. He hid in a tree and dropped nuts on Jethro's head.

66. True or False: Eb said he was glad he had deserted because war was such a horrifying experience.
    A. True
    B. False

67. True or False: Jethro had mixed feelings about harboring Eb. He knew Eb had been brave for two years and now was sick and needed help.
    A. True
    B. False

68. What did Jenny think was bothering Jethro?
    A. She thought he had been smoking and had made himself sick.
    B. She thought he was in love.
    C. She thought it was just puberty.
    D. She thought he was too preoccupied with thoughts of the war.

Across Five Aprils Multiple Choice Study Questions Page 15

69. What did Jethro do to solve his problem?
    A. He went to his minister for counseling.
    B. He went to see a lawyer.
    C. He asked Mr. Milton for advice.
    D. He wrote a letter to President Lincoln.

70. True or False: Jethro got a letter from General Grant that said all deserters were forgiven and could go home.
    A. True
    B. False

Across Five Aprils Multiple Choice Study Questions Page 16

Chapter 10

71. Who was Joe Hooker?
    A. He was a deserter who was making a nuisance of himself in the area.
    B. He was a general who created his own downfall.
    C. He was the new teacher who had come to replace Shad.
    D. He was a government agent who had been sent to look for spies in the area.

72. What did Shad's letter to Jenny say?
    A. He proposed to her.
    B. It said she should marry someone else because he no longer loved her.
    C. He asked her to wait for him no matter how long it took.
    F. It said she should prepare for the probability of heartbreak.

73. What did Eb do?
    A. He rejoined the army, dug ditches, and endured the scorn of the other soldiers.
    B. He ran away and joined the army of the South.
    C. He killed himself.
    D. He took on a new identity and moved West.

74. What were people's feelings about the battle at Gettysburg?
    A. They saw it as the turning point of the war.
    B. Most thought too many lives had been lost.
    C. They were glad for the victory but puzzled that the Union had given up the opportunity to crush Lee's army.
    D. They didn't think it was a very significant battle because it had been fought in the North. They thought the really important battles were fought in the South.

75. Why did Jenny go to Washington?
    A. She had been elected by the town to send a request for the end of the war to the President.
    B. She had been sent for by Shad's aunt because he was there in critical condition.
    C. She was going to go to nursing school.
    D. It was no longer safe for young women to be on the farms because of the bands of roving soldiers. Her parents sent her there for protection.

76. Was Jenny's trip to Washington worthwhile?
    A. Yes, it was.
    B. No, it wasn't.

Across Five Aprils Multiple Choice Study Questions Page 17

Chapter 11

77. What happened at Chicamauga?
    A. It was a victory for the North.
    B. It was a victory for the South.
    C. It was impossible to tell which side had won.
    D. It was the final battle of the war.

78. What was John upset about in his letter?
    A. The army was wasting supplies.
    B. He missed his family.
    C. His unit was treated like a third-rate unit and was teased by the others.
    D. He had not been paid for several months.

79. What comforted John?
    A. The thought that his one last brother was close to his boys comforted John.
    B. The fact that his father was still alive comforted John.
    C. Only the letters from Nancy gave him any comfort.
    D. He was counting the days until his tour of duty was up.

80. What did Shad think of General Grant?
    A. He had confidence that this man would win the war for the North.
    B He thought Grant was just another in a long line of poor generals.
    C. He reminded him of his uncle.
    D. He thought he was a wimp.

81. What did Shad think of McClellan's nomination for President?
    A. He didn't like it.
    B. He was pleased although he was still for Lincoln.
    C. He thought it was ludicrous.
    D. He didn't care one way or the other.

82. When did the North begin to rejoice?
    A. They began to rejoice after the battle in Atlanta.
    B. They began to rejoice after the battle in New Orleans.
    C. They began to rejoice after the battles in Mobile and Alabama.
    D. They began to rejoice after the battle in Fredricksburg.

83. True or False: Lincoln was re-elected because the people thought it would be bad luck to switch presidents in the middle of a war.
    A. True
    B. False

Across Five Aprils Multiple Choice Study Questions Page 18

84. What message did Bill send?
    A. He had defected to the North.
    B. He was hiding out in Colorado.
    C. He was in a hospital in Maryland.
    D. He was a prisoner in a Union camp, and he had not killed Tom.

Across Five Aprils Multiple Choice Study Questions Page 19

Chapter 12

85. What was Sherman's gift to Lincoln?
     A. It was the city of Savannah.
     B. It was the city of Baton Rouge.
     C. It was the city of Charleston.
     D. It was the city of Richmond.

86. What did Ed Turner think of the soldiers' looting?
     A. He thought they deserved whatever they could get because they had fought so long.
     B. He thought it was okay as long as they didn't take anything of his.
     C. He thought his son would lose the morals he had been taught.
     D. He thought they should be stopped immediately.

87. What were Ross Milton's thoughts about peace?
     A. An end to the war would create an immediate peace.
     B. There would never be peace as long as people still secretly supported the South.
     C. Men were not naturally peaceful creatures, and it wouldn't last. They would start another war somewhere else.
     D. Peace would be hard to come by, and the scars from the war would be a long time in healing.

88. True or False: Ross Martin was in favor of the thirteenth amendment, but he suspected that it would be decades before the reality of the dream would be realized.
     A. True
     B. False

89. What happened in the second week of April?
     A. Matt Creighton died.
     B. Jethro came of age.
     C. Jenny and Shad got married.
     D. The South surrendered to the North at Appomattox Court House in Virginia.

90. Who brought the news about Lincoln's death?
     A. Ellen heard it from a neighbor.
     B. Ross Milton drove to the farm to tell them.
     C. Nancy told them.
     D. Jethro read it in the newspaper.

91. True or False: While Jethro thought it was unfortunate that Lincoln had died, he also thought it was symbolic of a new beginning for the country.
     A. True
     B. False

Across Five Aprils Multiple Choice Study Questions Page 20

92. Who was the gaunt soldier Jethro found in the field?
    A. It was Bill.
    B. It was Eb.
    C. It was Shad.
    D. It was Travis.

93. What was planned for Jethro?
    A. He would move East and live with Jenny and Shad and go to school.
    B. He would take over the farm for his father.
    C. He would be sent to join the frontier army.
    D. He would learn the newspaper trade from Ross Milton.

ANSWER KEY - MULTIPLE CHOICE STUDY/QUIZ QUESTIONS
Across Five Aprils

Chapter 1	Chapter 2	Chapter 3
1. A	12. B	16. C
2. C	13. D	17. B
3. D	14. A	18. A
4. B	15. B	19. A
5. D		20. C
6. A		21. D
7. C		22. B
8. B		23. A
9. D		
10. A		
11. A		

Chapter 4	Chapter 5	Chapter 6
24. C	31. B	42. B
25. A	32. D	43. A
26. D	33. C	44. C
27. B	34. B	45. D
28. C	35. A	46. B
29. C	36. C	47. C
30. A	37. B	48. A
	38. A	49. D
	39. D	50. A
	40. D	
	41. C	

Chapters 7 & 8	Chapter 9	Chapter 10
51. C	62. D	71. B
52. B	63. A	72. D
53. A	64. B	73. A
54. D	65. C	74. C
55. C	66. D	75. B
56. B	67. B	76. A
57. D	68. A	
58. A	69. D	
59. B	70. C	
60. C		
61. B		

Chapter 11	Chapter 12
77. D	85. A
78. C	86. C
79. A	87. D
80. B	88. B
81. B	89. D
82. C	90. C
83. A	91. B
84. D	92. C
	93. A

PREREADING VOCABULARY WORKSHEETS

VOCABULARY - *Across Five Aprils*

<u>Chapters 1-2</u> Part I: Using Prior Knowledge and Contextual Clues

Below are the sentences in which the vocabulary words appear in the text. Read the sentence. Use any clues you can find in the sentence combined with your prior knowledge, and write what you think the underlined words mean on the lines provided.

1. . . . there were <u>reverberations</u> of Calvinism strong within her which would have protested vigorously against the vanity of regret for a passing beauty.

   _____

2. . . . [Yale] had known the frustration of trying to penetrate the <u>apathy</u> and unconcern of a backwoods classroom.

   _____

3. Jethro was depressed by her somber mood, but not by the <u>imminence</u> of war.

   _____

4. She was <u>amiable</u> but aloof to the friendly Creightons . . . .

   _____

5. Jethro, although he was concerned mostly about the goodness of the food he ate, was vaguely aware of a troubled <u>preoccupation</u> all about him.

   _____

6. . . . if tomorrow every slave in the South had his freedom and come up North, would yore <u>abolitionists</u> git the crocodile tears sloshed out of their eyes so they could take the black man by the hand?

   _____

7. Jethro felt as if he were bursting with the <u>tumult</u> inside him.

   _____

8. Jethro sank down on the ground, weak with <u>fatigue</u> and emotion . . . .

   _____

Vocabulary - *Across Five Aprils* Chapters 1-2 continued

Part II: Match the words and their definitions.

___ 1. reverberation A. something that engrosses the mind
___ 2. apathy B. people who wanted no more slavery
___ 3. imminence C. agitation of the mind or emotions; a disturbance
___ 4. preoccupation D. being physically or emotionally tired
___ 5. abolitionists E. indifference
___ 6. tumult F. the quality of being about to happen
___ 7. fatigue G. an echo-like effect

Vocabulary - *Across Five Aprils* Chapters 3-4

Part I: Using Prior Knowledge and Contextual Clues

Below are the sentences in which the vocabulary words appear in the text. Read the sentence. Use any clues you can find in the sentence combined with your prior knowledge, and write what you think the underlined words mean on the lines provided.

1. Miles of <u>bunting</u> draped dozens of platforms, where speakers . . . found themselves called upon to fan the wrath of the people.

   _____

2. The dust and heat, the emotion and noise, became almost unbearable to many; but there were always others who returned the following week, comforting their <u>baser</u> selves with barbecued pork and fowl, while their spirits were uplifted by words of high resolve and confidence from the speaker's platform.

   _____

3. Color was splashed through the woods as if it had been thrown about by some madcap <u>wastrel</u> who spilled out, during the weeks of one brief autumn, beauty enough to last for years.

   _____

4. He tried to imagine what the <u>ironclads</u> looked like and how they had taken Fort Henry . . . .

   _____

5. Ellen smiled <u>wanly</u> at his eagerness.

   _____

6. There might be another adjustment of his collar, another gift for Shad, more <u>admonitions</u> about his "comp'ny manners" . . . .

   _____

7. "A man has the right to the dignity of his own fireside after a day's work," he said, and he had allowed his sons and Shadrach to cut down trees from his own land for the <u>annex</u>.

   _____

8. . . . . I think he's overshooting the mark when he sets himself up as knowing exactly what is right or wrong for two other people. I think he's being <u>tyrannical</u> . . . .

   _____

9. Jethro did not understand the <u>allusion</u>, and Shadrach seemed to be in no mood for explanations.

   _____

Vocabulary - *Across Five Aprils* Chapters 3-4 continued

Part II: Determining the Meaning

You have tried to figure out the meanings of the vocabulary words for Chapter 3 & 4. Now match the vocabulary words to their dictionary definitions. If there are words for which you cannot figure out the definition by contextual clues and by process of elimination, look them up in a dictionary.

___ 8. bunting
___ 9. wastrel
___ 10. ironclads
___ 11. wanly
___ 12. admonitions
___ 13. annex
___ 14. tyrannical
___ 15. allusion

A. reprimands
B. oppressively domineering
C. indirect referenced
D. an addition or auxiliary building
E. strips of material in patriotic colors used for festive decorations
F. in a way showing one is tired or sad
G. one who wastes things
H. 19th century war ships having sides with metal plates as armor

Vocabulary - *Across Five Aprils* Chapter 5

Part I: Using Prior Knowledge and Contextual Clues
 Below are the sentences in which the vocabulary words appear in the text. Read the sentence. Use any clues you can find in the sentence combined with your prior knowledge, and write what you think the underlined words mean on the lines provided.

1. Jeth, we need coffee and a passel of other things from town.

_____

2. . . . the sun's rays barely got through the great bare branches that overlapped and intertwined above the narrow road.

_____

3. . . . there was no beauty in Newton to soften the view of muddy streets and the stark bleakness of bare trees

_____

4. The man looked as if he had lived in filth for a lifetime, and Jethro felt a loathing that was new to him.

_____

5. He looked directly at the man with an anger that dissipated his weakness.

_____

6. He turned belligerently when he reached the door.

_____

7. You're a very astute woman, Lily, but like most of us, you have your blind spots.

_____

8. She nodded caustically at that and stood surveying the two of them for a moment, her hands on her wide hips.

_____

9. . . . it floundered through the sour-smelling mud and over mammoth tree roots.

_____

10. Both man and boy seemed to be in tacit agreement that the attack at the bridge was a closed incident, a thing for which they felt a solid indifference.

_____

Vocabulary - *Across Five Aprils* Chapter 5 continued

Part II: Determining the Meaning

You have tried to figure out the meanings of the vocabulary words for Chapter 5. Now match the vocabulary words to their dictionary definitions. If there are words for which you cannot figure out the definition by contextual clues and by process of elimination, look them up in a dictionary.

___ 16. passel   A. defiantly; in a hostile manner
___ 17. stark   B. feeling of repulsion
___ 18. loathing   C. huge
___ 19. dissipated   D. capable of burning; in a fiery manner
___ 20. belligerently   E. a bunch; many
___ 21. astute   F. unspoken
___ 22. caustically   G. dispersed; sent or went away
___ 23. mammoth   H. bare; harsh; desolate
___ 24. tacit   I. shrewd; smart concerning one's own affairs

Vocabulary - *Across Five Aprils* Chapters 6-7

Part I: Using Prior Knowledge and Contextual Clues

Below are the sentences in which the vocabulary words appear in the text. Read the sentence. Use any clues you can find in the sentence combined with your prior knowledge, and write what you think the underlined words mean on the lines provided.

1. . . . or to know that hay, desperately needed for winter feeding, lay rotting in a wet quagmire of a field.

_____

2. "She ain't never bin selfish before," he thought. . . . "She's never been selfish before," he amended, and some of his anger was dissipated before the satisfaction of his new learning.

_____

3. He shivered a little. There was something ominous in the hoofbeats.

_____

4. It was the peak of the planting season, and the nights spent on the hard ground took their toll of men whose endurance was needed for the hard daily work in the fields.

_____

5. That was a kind of punishment favored by mobs and self-appointed judges--coal oil in the culprit's well.

_____

6. To the Patriots who defiled the well and burned the barn on Matthew Creighton's farm . . . .

_____

7. Jethro . . . had watched the fun from the sidelines, and that had been enough; some of the laughter and gaiety had overflowed to touch him, and he had felt himself a part of it.

_____

8. On the third night the ruffians struck. A back window was pried open, and the vandalism was proceeding in full force . . . .

_____

9. . . . a story that caused Wortman to be demoted, even by his own lieutenants, from the role of a swaggering desperado to that of an inept and ridiculous figure, whining in his misery.

_____

Vocabulary - *Across Five Aprils* Chapters 6-7 continued

Part II: Determining the Meaning
　　You have tried to figure out the meanings of the vocabulary words for Chapters 6 & 7. Now match the vocabulary words to their dictionary definitions. If there are words for which you cannot figure out the definition by contextual clues and by process of elimination, look them up in a dictionary.

___ 25. quagmire
___ 26. amended
___ 27. ominous
___ 28. endurance
___ 29. culprits
___ 30. defiled
___ 31. gaiety
___ 32. ruffians
___ 33. desperado

A. strength over a long period of time
B. festivity; happiness
C. delinquents; muggers; gangsters
D. soft, muddy land
E. desperate outlaw
F. polluted
G. fixed, corrected
H. threatening
I. people charged with crimes

Vocabulary - *Across Five Aprils* Chapters 8-9

Part I: Using Prior Knowledge and Contextual Clues
    Below are the sentences in which the vocabulary words appear in the text. Read the sentence. Use any clues you can find in the sentence combined with your prior knowledge, and write what you think the underlined words mean on the lines provided.

1. "Be glad you're a boy, young feller, and don't hev to pester yoreself with all these troubles that men be sufferin' through these days," he said genially.

_____

2. I tell you frankly that the contagion of their devotion has not yet gripped me.

_____

3. men who knew what gangrenous wounds were like . . . .

_____

4. For a few seconds Jethro forgot the Federal Registrars and the fact that not only the word which preceded Eb, but his method of announcing himself gave credence to the suspicion that he was a deserter.

_____

5. . . . how could loyalty to these men be true if one were going to harbor and give comfort to a man who simply said, "I quit."

_____

6. Eb's often reiterated, "I'll be goin' on soon, Jeth; I won't be a burden to you much longer," became like the whippoorwill's cry--always the same and never ending.

_____

7. . . . still a sheltered young boy who did the tasks his father set for him and shunned the idea that he dare think for himself.

_____

8. . . . so involved as to present a situation in which a solution becomes agonizingly difficult.

_____

9. . . . and I pray that the remorse and despair which he has known since the time of his desertion will bring his better self to the cause for which so many of his young compatriots have laid down their lives.

_____

Vocabulary - *Across Five Aprils* Chapters 8-9 continued

Part II: Determining the Meaning
　　You have tried to figure out the meanings of the vocabulary words for Chapters 8 & 9. Now match the vocabulary words to their dictionary definitions. If there are words for which you cannot figure out the definition by contextual clues and by process of elimination, look them up in a dictionary.

___ 34. genially
___ 35. contagion
___ 36. gangrenous
___ 37. tethered
___ 38. credence
___ 39. harbor
___ 40. reiterated
___ 41. shunned
___ 42. agonizingly
___ 43. compatriots

A. believability
B. deliberately avoided
C. said or did something repeatedly
D. a bad influence; the spreading of an idea
E. people from one's own country or team
F. with great pain or difficulty
G. having decaying bodily tissues
H. tied with a short rope or string
I. to shelter
J. kindly; pleasantly

Vocabulary - *Across Five Aprils* Chapters 10 - 12

Part I: Using Prior Knowledge and Contextual Clues

    Below are the sentences in which the vocabulary words appear in the text. Read the sentence. Use any clues you can find in the sentence combined with your prior knowledge, and write what you think the underlined words mean on the lines provided.

1. "Fighting Joe Hooker" he was called, an arrogant man, highly <u>contemptuous</u> of McClellan and Burnside . . . .

_____

2. . . . . Vicksburg, perched high on the bluffs of the Mississippi, had natural fortification that Grant, with his <u>inept</u> stupidity, could not successfully storm . . . .

_____

3. The news of the battle was confused at first, <u>incoherent</u>, sometimes contradictory . . . .

_____

4. There had been a time when Matt Creighton <u>brooked</u> no criticism of a teacher from his children . . . .

_____

5. . . . the snipers located all long the slopes of Lookout Mountain and Missionary Ridge made it impossible for a wagonload of food or <u>provender</u> to get through to either men or animals.

_____

6. Then finally the command came for them to take the front-line trenches at the base of Missionary Ridge, which towered like a steep wall opposite Lookout. That was when <u>pandemonium</u> broke out.

_____

7. But they did hold on, and as the war trailed drearily on, <u>vindictiveness</u> toward the stubborn stand of the seceding states grew steadily more bitter in the North.

_____

8. The <u>preponderance</u> of the soldier vote was for Lincoln that year.

_____

9. . . . it was then that South Carolina knew the lash of a triumphant army drunk with the plundering of Georgia and enraged at the stubborn <u>tenacity</u> of the South in holding onto a cause that was already lost.

_____

Vocabulary - *Across Five Aprils* Chapters 10-12 continued

10. Then March came, breaking the back of winter with warmth <u>permeating</u> the cold . . . .

_____

Part II: Determining the Meaning

You have tried to figure out the meanings of the vocabulary words for Chapters 10 - 12. Now match the vocabulary words to their dictionary definitions. If there are words for which you cannot figure out the definition by contextual clues and by process of elimination, look them up in a dictionary.

___ 44. contemptuous
___ 45. inept
___ 46. incoherent
___ 47. brooked
___ 48. provender
___ 49. pandemonium
___ 50. vindictiveness
___ 51. preponderance
___ 52. tenacity
___ 53. permeating

A. food for animals
B. wild uproar
C. holding or sticking to something persistently
D. revengefulness
E. scornful
F. penetrating; spreading throughout
G. tolerated
H. majority
I. disjointed; not in an orderly manner
J. incompetent

ANSWER KEY - VOCABULARY
Across Five Aprils

Chapters 1-2
1. G
2. E
3. F
4. A
5. B
6. C
7. D

Chapters 3-4
8. E
9. G
10. H
11. F
12. A
13. D
14. B
15. C

Chapter 5
16. E
17. H
18. B
19. G
20. A
21. I
22. D
23. C
24. F

Chapters 6-7
25. D
26. G
27. H
28. A
29. I
30. F
31. B
32. C
33. E

Chapters 8-9
34. J
35. D
36. G
37. H
38. A
39. I
40. C
41. B
42. F
43. E

Chapters 10 - 12
44. E
45. J
46. I
47. G
48. A
49. B
50. D
51. H
52. C
53. F

DAILY LESSONS

LESSON ONE

Objectives
1. To introduce *Across Five Aprils*
2. To distribute books and other related materials

NOTE: Prior to this lesson, you need to have invited a guest speaker. Almost every state has a group of Civil War buffs who re-enact battles and have costumes. Check with your local historical society, museums, or chamber of commerce to find the contact people for the group in your state. If your state has no such group, the historical society should be able to tell you the names of some people in your area who are Civil War buffs. If not, check with the universities in your area--they usually have someone on staff who is very knowledgeable about the Civil War. If all else fails, find a good film about the Civil War as an introduction to the book, *Across Five Aprils*.

Activity #1
    Invite a guest speaker in to discuss the background for the American Civil War. Concentrate primarily on the causes of the war and its effects on the nation. Students will research information about the specific battles and the leaders of the armies, so you need not spend much time on those specifics in the introduction.

Activity #2
    Tell students that they are to preview the study questions, do the related vocabulary work, and read chapters one and two prior to Lesson Three. (Give students a day and date.)

Activity #3
    Distribute the materials for the unit: books, study guides, reading assignment sheets, etc. Explain to students how they should use these materials.

    Study Guides Students should read the study guide questions for each reading assignment prior to beginning the reading assignment to get a feeling for what events and ideas are important in the section they are about to read. After reading the section, students will (as a class or individually) answer the questions to review the important events and ideas from that section of the book. Students should keep the study guides as study materials for the unit test.

    Vocabulary Prior to reading a reading assignment, students will do vocabulary work related to the section of the book they are about to read. Following the completion of the reading of the book, there will be a vocabulary review of all the words used in the vocabulary assignments. Students should keep their vocabulary work as study materials for the unit test.

<u>Reading Assignment Sheet</u>   You need to fill in the reading assignment sheet to let students know by when their reading has to be completed. You can either write the assignment sheet up on a side blackboard or bulletin board and leave it there for students to see each day, or you can "ditto" copies for each student to have. In either case, you should advise students to become very familiar with the reading assignments so they know what is expected of them.

<u>Extra Activities Center</u>   The resource section of this unit contains suggestions for an extra library of related books and articles in your classroom as well as crossword and word search puzzles. Make an extra activities center in your room where you will keep these materials for students to use. (Bring the books and articles in from the library and keep several copies of the puzzles on hand.) Explain to students that these materials are available for students to use when they finish reading assignments or other class work early.

<u>Nonfiction Assignment Sheet</u>   Explain to students that they each are to read at least one non-fiction piece from the in-class library at some time during the unit. The research they will do at the beginning of the unit may be used to fulfill this requirement. Students will fill out a nonfiction assignment sheet after completing the reading to help you evaluate their reading experiences and to help the students think about and evaluate their own reading experiences.

<u>Books</u>   Each school has its own rules and regulations regarding student use of school books. Advise students of the procedures that are normal for your school.

LESSON TWO

Objectives
1. To give students the opportunity to practice doing research
2. To help students get the places and players for the Civil War straight prior to reading *Across Five Aprils*
3. To have students assume the responsibilities required by working in a group

Activity #1

Take students to the library. Divide your class into three groups. One group will be The Places, another will be The People, and the third group will be The Map.

Give The People group a list of names of people who were important at the time of the American Civil War. (These are the people who are mentioned in *Across Five Aprils*.) They are to divide the list among themselves, assigning a number of "people" to each group member. Each member should research his "people" and should plan to give an oral report highlighting the essence of their importance in one minute or less during the next class period.

Give The Places group a list of names of places which were important during the Civil War. (These are the places which are mentioned in *Across Five Aprils*.) The group members are to divide the list of places among themselves, assigning a number of places to each group member. Each member should research his places and should plan to give an oral report highlighting the essence of their importance in one minute or less during the next class period.

Give The Map group a list of places that were important during the Civil War and/or were mentioned in the book *Across Five Aprils*. Also give this group a map of the United States on which they can mark their places. The members of the group should divide up the list of places among themselves, assigning a number of places to each group member. Each member should research the location of his places and be able to locate them on the group's map. In addition, students should divide up the states among the group members and each group member should find out some basic information about his/her assigned state's(s') role(s) in the war. Prior to Lesson Four this group must complete one map showing all the locations of the places on their list.

Explain to students that in Lesson Four (give students a day and date) they will be responsible for giving oral information about their research. The People and The Places groups are limited to one minute per person or place. Map group members must point out the locations of the places mentioned in the oral reports as they are being given.

Activity #2

Give the students this class period to complete their research.

GROUP ASSIGNMENT LISTS

The People

Lincoln	Fremont	McClellan	Jefferson Davis
Robert E. Lee	Pike	Sigel	Ulysses S. Grant
Van Dorn	Sherman	Halleck	Wm. Lloyd Garrison
John Brown	Pope	Longstreet	Burnside
Rosencrans	Bragg	Joe Hooker	Beauregard
Pemberton	Hood	Buell	Stonewall Jackson
George Thomas	Sheridan		Army of Cumberland
			Army of Tennessee
			Army of Potomac

The Places

Fort Sumter	Bull Run	Wilson's Creek	Ball's Bluff
Fort Henry	Donelson	Pea Ridge	Shiloh
Pittsburgh Landing	Corinth	Antietam	Fredericksburg
Stones River	Chancellorsville	Gettysburg	Vicksburg
Lookout Mountain	Atlanta	Chickamauga	Richmond
Missionary Ridge	Cedar Creek	Appomattox	Washington

The Map

Mark each state as Union, Confederate, or Border. (Mark only the states which were states in 1860-1865.)

Locate each of the above places on the map.

Locate these rivers: Tennessee, Ohio, Cumberland, and Mississippi on the map.

Locate each of these towns in Illinois: Olney, Newton, and Hildago.

LESSON THREE

Objectives
1. To review the main ideas and events of chapters 1-3
2. To help prepare students for their oral reports
3. To give students the opportunity to practice writing to inform
4. To give the teacher the opportunity to evaluate students' writing skills

Activity #1

Do the study guide for chapters 1-2 in class together. Ask the questions and let the students answer. Allow time for any necessary discussion. Write the correct answers to the questions on the board or overhead projector so students can copy them down for study use.

TEACHER'S NOTE: Depending on the students, I have let different students write the answers on the board or even ask the questions to lead the group. I would then jump in as necessary to guide the discussion. Use whatever techniques your particular students will handle best.

If you want to give your students a quiz on the material to make sure they did the required reading or to test their understanding of the reading prior to discussion, use the study questions (either short answer or multiple choice) as a short quiz and then discuss the answers.

Activity #2

Tell students that prior to Lesson Five (give students a day and a date) they should preview the study questions, do the prereading vocabulary worksheet, and complete the reading for chapters 3-4.

Activity #3

Distribute Writing Assignment #1. Discuss the directions in detail and give students ample time to complete the assignment. If students finish early, they may begin on the assignment made in Activity #2.

WRITING ASSIGNMENT #1 - *Across Five Aprils*

PROMPT
You have been assigned to find information about a person or place relating to the Civil War, and you will soon be asked to give a short oral presentation about the information you have found. To help you prepare for that presentation, you are to write a composition about the information you found. If you were assigned more than one person or place, you now will need to choose one person or place to write about.

PREWRITING
Most of your prewriting was done in the last class period when you did your research. Now look at the notes you took and organize them into a logical sequence. If you researched a person, you should have background information, information about his/her life during the war, and information about the person's life after the war (unless the person was killed during the war). If you researched a place, you should have background information about the place and information about what happened at that place during the war.

DRAFTING
Write an introductory paragraph in which you introduce your person or place and give basic background information.
  Write a paragraph about that person/place during the war.
  Write a concluding paragraph about the person/place after the war.

PROMPT
When you finish the rough draft of your paper, ask a student who sits near you to read it. After reading your rough draft, he/she should tell you what he/she liked best about your work, which parts were difficult to understand, and ways in which your work could be improved. Reread your paper considering your critic's comments and make the corrections you think are necessary.

PROOFREADING
Do a final proofreading of your paper double-checking your grammar, spelling, organization, and the clarity of your ideas.

LESSON FOUR

Objectives
1. To check students' group work
2. To give all students the background information produced by the group work
3. To give students the opportunity to practice public speaking
4. To show students that the places mentioned in their research and in *Across Five Aprils* really do exist

Activity
During this class period, have students give oral summaries of their research about the places and people from their lists. Allow approximately one minute per person/place. That will give students enough time to state the most important information and will keep this from becoming a week-long event. (After all, volumes have been written about each one of these!)

As students give their oral reports, all students in the class should jot down a few notes about each of the places/people on their Civil War Fact Worksheets. This will give students a quick reference guide to use as they read.

LESSON FIVE

Objectives
1. To review the main ideas and events from chapters 3-4
2. To complete the oral reports
3. To preview the study questions and vocabulary for chapter 5

Activity #1
Do the study guide questions for chapters 3-4 together in class. Again, if you wish to give your students a quiz, use the study guide questions in either format and then discuss the answers together.

Activity #2
Tell students that prior to the next class period they should preview the study questions and do the related prereading vocabulary worksheet for chapter 5.

Activity #3
Continue and complete the oral presentations students began in the last class period.

LESSON SIX

Objectives
1. To read chapter 5
2. To evaluate students' reading skills
3. To preview the study questions and vocabulary for chapters 6-7
4. To read chapters 6-7

Activity #1
Have students read chapter 5 orally. Each students should read a short passage from the chapter. If you have not yet given students a grade for oral reading this marking period, this would be a good opportunity to do so. An evaluation form is enclosed for your convenience.

Activity #2
Tell students that prior to Lesson Eight (give students a day/date), they should preview the study questions, do the related prereading vocabulary worksheet, and read chapters 6-7. If any time remains in this class period, students should begin this assignment.

LESSON SEVEN

Objectives
1. To give students the opportunity to write expressing their own opinions
2. To give the teacher the opportunity to evaluate students' writing skills
3. To remind students of their right and obligation to communicate with the officials they will elect

Activity #1
Distribute Writing Assignment #2. Discuss the directions in detail and give students ample time to complete the assignment.

Activity #2
While students are working on the writing assignment, call individual students to your desk or some other private area for a writing conference. Use the first writing assignment as a basis for your conference. Tell the student the best points about the composition and suggest ways the composition could have been improved. An evaluation form is enclosed for your convenience. Students should rewrite their first writing assignments taking your suggestions into consideration. Tell them when these revisions are due to be handed in.

(When grading the revisions, you may use an A-C-E scale: A=all revisions done correctly, C=some revisions done correctly, E=no revisions done or all done incorrectly. This will greatly speed your grading time and still give students credit for their work. As always, the more comments you can make to the students, the better.)

If students finish Writing Assignment #2 before the end of the period, they should work on their revisions or on the reading assignment made in the last class period.

ORAL READING EVALUATION - *Across Five Aprils*

Name _____ Class____ Date _____

SKILL	EXCELLENT	GOOD	AVERAGE	FAIR	POOR
Fluency	5	4	3	2	1
Clarity	5	4	3	2	1
Audibility	5	4	3	2	1
Pronunciation	5	4	3	2	1
_____	5	4	3	2	1
_____	5	4	3	2	1

Total ____ Grade ____

Comments:

WRITING EVALUATION FORM - *Across Five Aprils*

Name _____ Date _____

Grade _____

Circle One For Each Item:

Grammar: corrections noted on paper

Spelling: corrections noted on paper

Punctuation: corrections noted on paper

Legibility: excellent   good   fair   poor

_____   excellent   good   fair   poor

_____   excellent   good   fair   poor

Strengths:

Weaknesses:

Comments/Suggestions:

WRITING ASSIGNMENT #2 - *Across Five Aprils*

PROMPT

Jethro was concerned, wrote to President Lincoln, and got a reply. Often we forget that we have the right--even an obligation--to express our opinions to our elected officials: to inquire about things that concern us, to tell them how we feel about issues that are important to us, to let them know when we think they are doing a good job, and to let them know when we think they are not doing what we think they should. If our voices are silent, we are not contributing to having a successful democracy.

Your assignment is to write a letter to an elected government official for one of the purposes mentioned in the paragraph above.

PREWRITING

First decide why you are going to write a letter. Is there something that's bugging you? Do you want more information about a particular project or topic? Do you have a complaint? Were you particularly impressed with something you heard in the news lately?

Next, decide to whom your letter would best be addressed. If you're concerned about a local issue, write to local officials. If your inquiry or comment concerns your state, write to your state officials. If your inquiry or comment concerns the nation, write to your national officials. Your teacher can supply you with the names and addresses of the appropriate authorities.

Make a list of the points you want to make to the official. Next to each point jot down a few notes of explanation or examples to illustrate your point.

DRAFTING

Begin your letter in a formal letter format, including the inside address. Write one short paragraph in which you introduce the topic of your letter and state your main point.

Write one paragraph for each of the points you wish to make. Use examples to illustrate your point or make a further explanation to make your point clear within each paragraph.

Write a paragraph of conclusion in which you thank the official for reading your letter and ask for a speedy reply (if a reply is requested).

Close and sign your letter.

PROMPT

When you finish the rough draft of your paper, ask a student who sits near you to read it. After reading your rough draft, he/she should tell you what he/she liked best about your work, which parts were difficult to understand, and ways in which your work could be improved. Reread your paper considering your critic's comments and make the corrections you think are necessary.

PROOFREADING

Do a final proofreading of your paper double-checking your grammar, spelling, organization, and the clarity of your ideas.

LESSON EIGHT

Objectives
1. To review the main ideas and events from chapters 5-7
2. To preview the study questions and do the prereading vocabulary work for chapters 8-9
3. To read chapters 8-9

Activity #1
Discuss the study guide questions for chapters 5-7. Write the answers on the board for students to copy for study use.

Activity #2
Give students about fifteen minutes to preview the study questions and do the vocabulary worksheet for chapters 8-9.

Activity #3
Have students read chapters 8-9. If you did not complete the oral reading evaluations in Lesson Six, this is a good chance to do so. Otherwise, if you have completed the evaluations, students may work on this reading assignment silently.

LESSON NINE

Objectives
1. To review the main events and ideas from chapters 8-9
2. To take a break from the read-and-question routine
3. To review the basics of good grammar

Activity #1
Do the study guide for chapters 8-9 in class together. Ask the questions and let the students answer. Allow time for any necessary discussion. Write the correct answers to the questions on the board or overhead projector so students can copy them down for study use.

Activity #2
Distribute the Grammar Worksheet. Give students ample time to complete this assignment and then discuss the answers in detail.

Activity #3
Tell students that prior to the next class meeting they should preview the study questions and do the prereading vocabulary worksheet for chapters 10-12.

GRAMMAR WORKSHEET - *Across Five Aprils*

Correct the grammatical and spelling errors in the following passages from *Across Five Aprils*:

Dere Fokes:

    I take pencle in hand to let you no that Eb and me is alright.

    I expect you no by now how we took Fort Henry down here. Mebby I oughtnt say we took it becus it was the ironclads that done it. Old admiral Foote had what it took and he give the rebs a dressin down but some of his iron-clads got hit hard. A boy i no was on the Essex and he was burned so bad he dide when that boat got nocked out of the fite.

    Us boys didnt do much fitin at Fort Henry but at Donelson I can tell you we made up fer it. We had done a foolish thing on our way to Donelson and I will rite you about it. When we was marchin tord the fort the weather was like a hot april day back home. We was feelin set-up about Fort Henry and when some of the boys got tard of carryin hevey blanket rolls they jest up and throwed em away. Then more and more of us acted like crazy fools and we throwed away hevey cotes and things to make our lodes a littel liter. As soon as we got to Donelson the wether turned cold as Billy Sideways and some of the boys that was sick or bad hurt they froze to deth in the snow. Things was awful bad with so many kilt and others froze. I felt sick when I looked at them and so I am not so proud about Donelson as mebby I ought to be. I miss yore good cookin Ma. You tell Jeth that bein a soljer aint so much.

                  yrs truely

                    Tom

... We et things that wood make you sick to think about and the pore horses and mules was as despert hongry as we was. ...

.... It aint that we was so much apantin to fite, wed had aplenty of fitin. Still we didnt like it of Grant to give us the easy post and hev the Potomac and Tennessee boys lookin at us like we was a third rate army. If youve read of Hookers boys afitin the battel up on Lookout you kno that it was fine. They licked the rebs up ther and we had to admit that they done what we hadnt. But you shood a seen Joe Hooker strut . . . .

LESSON TEN

Objective
    To complete reading the novel

Activity
    Have students read chapters 10-12 either orally or silently in class.

LESSONS ELEVEN AND TWELVE

Objectives
    1. To prepare students for a discussion of the novel
    2. To check students' understanding of the novel
    3. To give the teacher the opportunity to evaluate students' writing skills

Activity #1
    Do the study questions for chapters 10-12.

Activity #2
    Assign one of the Extra Discussion Questions/Writing Assignments to each of your students. Advise students that they will be responsible for leading a class discussion about the questions they have been assigned. Give students ample time to prepare their answers.

Activity #3
    Have each student lead a discussion he/she was assigned. Use these responses as springboards for class discussions of the topics suggested by the questions. Jump in as necessary to guide the discussion and to add important points the students may have missed.

NOTE: Since there are so many discussion questions and since some of the topics involved may take a substantial amount of time to discuss in depth, I suggest that you allow two class periods for this activity.

EXTRA WRITING ASSIGNMENTS/DISCUSSION QUESTIONS - *Across Five Aprils*

Interpretation

1. From what point of view is *Across Five Aprils* written, and what effect does that have on the story?

2. Is the story of *Across Five Aprils* believable? Explain why or why not.

3. Where is the climax of the story? Explain your choice.

4. Are the characters in *Across Five Aprils* stereotypes? If so, explain the usefulness of employing stereotypes in the novel. If they are not, explain how they merit individuality.

5. What is the setting of the story? Could this story have been set in a different time and place and still have the same effect?

6. What are the conflicts in the story? Are the conflicts all resolved? If so, how? If not, why not?

7. Trace public opinion of Lincoln, Grant, and McClellan through the story and tell the events which caused public opinion to change.

8. What arguments are put forth in the story to explain the causes of the American Civil War?

Critical

9. Describe the relationships between Jethro and the following people: Bill, John, Shad, Jenny, and Eb.

10. Explore the use of the romantic view of war and the realistic view of war in *Across Five Aprils*.

11. Explain the role of death in the story.

12. Explain the role of education in *Across Five Aprils*.

13. Explain the importance of each of the following minor characters: Jake Roscoe, Dan Lawrence, Hig Phillips, Dave Burdow, Wilse Graham, Guy Wortman, Ed Turner, Nancy, and the little boys.

14. Explain the importance/significance of Walnut Hill.

15. Give a complete character analysis of Ellen Creighton.

Across Five Aprils Extra Discussion Questions page 2

16. Explain how *Across Five Aprils* could be considered a book about individualism.

17. Compare and contrast Jenny and Nancy.

18. One of the things that makes *Across Five Aprils* an interesting book is that there are several stories within the main story. What are they, and how are they held together in the main story line?

19. Explain the use of foreshadowing in *Across Five Aprils*.

20. Explain how Irene Hunt uses color in *Across Five Aprils*.

21. Characterize Irene Hunt's style of writing.

22. How does the author use details to add to the depth and effect of the story?

23. Explain the use of darkness, night, and nightmares in *Across Five Aprils*.

24. What is the use of having characters who never have any lines in the story (the dead children and Mary, the eldest son gone to California, and Travis Burdow, for example)?

25. Why was grammar so important to Jethro; why did he take the time to study Mr. Milton's book?

Personal Response
26. Did you enjoy reading *Across Five Aprils*? Why or why not?

27. Explain how *Across Five Aprils* shows how the Civil War affected family unity, particularly in the "border states."

28. *Across Five Aprils* was published in 1964. In the book, Mr. Milton said, ". . . after the thirteenth amendment has become a part of our Constitution and for years afterward--twenty-five, maybe fifty--there will be men and women with dark faces who will walk the length and width of this land in search of the bright promise the thirteenth amendment holds out to them." Explain the relevance of Mr. Milton's words at the time that this book was published and today.

29. Explain how *Across Five Aprils* is a story about growing up and growing older.

30. Is the United States likely to have another civil war? If so, why? If not, why not?

LESSON THIRTEEN

Objective
    To review all of the vocabulary work done in this unit

Activity
    Choose one (or more) of the vocabulary review activities listed below and spend your class period as directed in the activity. Some of the materials for these review activities are located in the Vocabulary Resources section in this unit.

VOCABULARY REVIEW ACTIVITIES

1. Divide your class into two teams and have an old-fashioned spelling or definition bee.

2. Give each of your students (or students in groups of two, three or four) an *Across Five Aprils* Vocabulary Word Search Puzzle. The person (group) to find all of the vocabulary words in the puzzle first wins.

3. Give students an *Across Five Aprils* Vocabulary Word Search Puzzle without the word list. The person or group to find the most vocabulary words in the puzzle wins.

4. Use an *Across Five Aprils* Vocabulary Crossword Puzzle. Put the puzzle onto a transparency on the overhead projector (so everyone can see it), and do the puzzle together as a class.

5. Give students an *Across Five Aprils* Vocabulary Matching Worksheet to do.

6. Divide your class into two teams. Use *Across Five Aprils* vocabulary words with their letters jumbled as a word list. Student 1 from Team A faces off against Student 1 from Team B. You write the first jumbled word on the board. The first student (1A or 1B) to unscramble the word wins the chance for his/her team to score points. If 1A wins the jumble, go to student 2A and give him/her a definition. He/she must give you the correct spelling of the vocabulary word which fits that definition. If he/she does, Team A scores a point, and you give student 3A a definition for which you expect a correctly spelled matching vocabulary word. Continue giving Team A definitions until some team member makes an incorrect response. An incorrect response sends the game back to the jumbled-word face off, this time with students 2A and 2B. Instead of repeating giving definitions to the first few students of each team, continue with the student after the one who gave the last incorrect response on the team. For example, if Team B wins the jumbled-word face-off, and student 5B gave the last incorrect answer for Team B, you would start this round of definition questions with student 6B, and so on. The team with the most points wins!

7. Have students write a story in which they correctly use as many vocabulary words as possible. Have students read their compositions orally! Post the most original compositions on your bulletin board.

LESSON FOURTEEN

Objectives
1. To check students' understanding of the novel
2. To give the teacher the opportunity to evaluate students' writing skills
3. To give students the opportunity to practice writing to persuade

Activity #1

Distribute Writing Assignment #3. Discuss the directions in detail and give students ample time to complete the assignment.

LESSON FIFTEEN

Objectives
1. To show students an actual newspaper page from the Civil War era
2. To show students an actual account of a battle of the Civil War that was written within days after the battle happened
3. To show students the deep-rooted conflicts that existed during the Civil War

NOTE: No matter what newspaper or articles we would choose for this exercise, someone would probably be offended. We have, therefore, chosen one of our local papers from Worcester County, Maryland. Since Maryland was a border state, some people were pro-North and others were pro-South. Worcester County is located on the southern part of the Eastern Shore of Maryland. Being so situated, one would think that the newspaper would be pro-Confederacy, but it wasn't. It was pro-Union. On the other hand, it showed definite Southern convictions regarding the issue of Abolitionism. The *Worcester County Shield* is used in this exercise because the newspaper was readily accessible to this author and because this newspaper expressed both Northern and Southern views on various issues.

There were only two copies of the newspaper left for this era, one from 1891 and one from 1863. We have re-created the front page stories from each issue. In the original newspapers, there were some misspellings/typographical errors and some of the words were illegible due to the condition of the papers.

We didn't have room on one letter-sized page to print everything that was on the full-sized newspaper page. What we have done is recreated a representative sample of the kinds of things that were included in the newspaper. The copy is taken directly, word-for-word, from the newspaper. We have left out several advertisements and legal notices (property for sale, bankruptcy notices, etc.) which were not important to the purposes of this assignment.

SUGGESTION: Since the type face on these newspaper pages is so small, it might be a good idea to make transparencies of the pages and to use the overhead projector to show students the pages. You are free, however, to make paper copies of the pages if you wish.

Lesson Fifteen Continued

Activity

Remind students that Jethro often read the newspaper in *Across Five Aprils*. Explain to students that you thought it might be fun and interesting for them to see actual newspapers from the Civil War era. Distribute the two newspaper pages or show them on your overhead projector. Explain the appropriate information from the NOTE above.

Read through the articles with your students. Have students determine which things were pro-North and which things were pro-South. Discuss the articles and the kinds of things that were printed in the newspaper: news stories, editorials, fiction, advertisements, public notices, etc.

Worcester County Shield

VOL. XVIIL--NO. 34.　　SNOW HILL, MD, SATURDAY MORNING, AUG. 22, 1863

Worcester County Shield
Published every Saturday
by B. EVERETT SMITH

TERMS OF SUBSCRIPTION
TWO DOLLARS a year, invariably in arrears, to be paid within one month from the date of subscription. No papers will be given to any person except subscribers or advertisers.

THE LAW OF NEWSPAPERS
1. Subscribers who do not give express notice to the contrary are considered as wishing to continue their subscriptions.
2. If subscribers order the discontinuance of their papers, the publisher can continue to send them until arrears are paid.
3. If subscribers neglect or refuse to take their papers from the office to which they are directed, they are held responsible till they settle their bills, and order the paper discontinued.

THE WASHINGTON HOTEL

SNOW HILL, Maryland
EDWARD J. HENRY,
Proprietor

This large House, corner of Washington and Green streets, is in complete order for the accommodation of the public, and the Proprietor would respectfully inform those who may be pleased to patronize his establishment that no efforts will be spared to give satisfaction to his guests,-- by strict attention thereto he hopes to render the WASHINGTON HOUSE at all times agreeable to its patrons.

PROSPECTUS
The New York Daily News

is devoted to PEACE,
Politics, News, the Arts, Science, Literature, the dissemination of useful Intelligence, and the preservation of a REPUBLICAN FORM OF GOVERNMENT. It is hostile to all USURPATIONS OF AUTHORITY, to all encroachment upon the PRIVILEGES OF AMERICAN CITIZENSHIP. It is a firm and fearless supporter of CONSTITUTIONAL LIBERTY, the RIGHTS OF THE PEOPLE and of the STATES. A Weekly Edition is issued on every Saturday.
BENJAMIN WOOD, Editor and Proprietor.
Daily Edition Per Annum　Six Dollars
Daily Edition 6 Months Three Dollars
Daily Edition Single Copy Two Cents
Weekly Edition Per Annum One Dollar

Tudor & Townsend

PRODUCE & COMMISSION
MERCHANTS
133 W. Pratt St., Opposite Bowly's Wharf.
For the Sale of
GRAIN, FLOUR, TOBACCO,
SEEDS, PROVISIONS
and Country Produce Generally. ALSO a large assortment of
FRUIT & ORNAMENTAL TREES

TRUSSES, SHOULDER BRACES.
ELASTIC STOCKINGS FOR
ENLARGED VEINS OF THE
LEG &C.,:
INSTRUMENTS FOR ALL

DEFORMITIES.
DR. GLOVER'S
New Lever Truss

has taken the place of other Trusses for the retention and cure of Hernia or Ruptage. Acting upon the principle of a lever, it never loses its strength.

A War Novel

Speaking of the love-light and the ravishing romance of life's young dream, to use the language of Baker the Hoker, we are reminded of the latest and greatest "Nashional" production of the day. Possessing imagery and poetic diction, to say nothing of the loyal foundation of the Laureate, we can safely say that it is worthy the heart, head and pen of Baker the Joker. This specimen brick of current literature is entitled

BARKER THE YOUNG PATRIOT
Chapter 1.

"No, William Barker, you cannot have my daughter's hand in marriage until you are her equal in wealth and social position."

The speaker was a haughty old man of some sixty years, and the person whom he addressed was a fine-looking young man of twenty-one.

With a sad aspect the young man withdrew from the stately mansion.

Chapter 2.

Six months later the young man stood in the presence of the haughty old man.

"What! you here again!" angrily cried the old man.

"Ay, old man," proudly exclaimed Wm. Barker. "I am here, your daughter's equal and yours!"

The old man's lips curled with scorn. A derisive smile lit up his cold features; when, casting violently upon the marble centre-table an enormous roll of greenbacks, William Barker cried--

"See! Look on this wealth. And I've ten-fold more. Listen, old man! You turned me from your door. But I did not despair. I secured a contract for furnishing the Army of the Potomac with beef--"

"Yes, yes!" eagerly exclaimed the old man.

"And I bought up all the disabled calvary horses I could find."

"I see! I see!" cried the old man. "And good beef they make, too."

"They do! They do! And the profits are immense."

"I should say so!"

"And now, sir, I claim your daughter's fair hand."

"Boy, she is yours. But hold! Look me in the eye. Throughout all this have you been loyal?"

"To the core!" cried William Barker.

"And," continued the old man in a voice husky with emotion, "you are in favor of a vigorous prosecution of the war?"

"I am! I am!"

"Then, boy, take her! Maria, child, come hither. Your William claims thee. Be happy, my children! and whatever our lot in life may be, let us all support the Government.

OAT STRAW AS FOOD FOR SICK

"I have often noticed," says Dr. Dadd, "that sick horses will eat oat straw in preference to any other kind of fodder, as a matter of course, however, some will refuse to eat it. Oat straw contains a vast amount of untrimental matter and some phosphates, and when converted into a sort of bran by means of millstones, is a very nourishing diet.--This sort of thing is useful when combined with ground gnats, for animals whose systems lack the exquisite amount of phosphates. A milch cow, for instance, the subject of prostrating disease, is very much benefited by food of this kind.

THE EVIL SIGNS

One of the most ominous signs of the times is the fact that our military successes bring out to new force the old abolition notions which have been cherished by designing agitators for many years, but which others, professing more moderate views, and less courageous, though actuated by the same sentiments, have not dared to confess. To these men, victory is not so much the harbinger of peace as affording ground for more exacting demands in the interests of abolitionists, as conditions of settlement.-- They would not consent to a settlement with the old Union as a basis. We say this in no partisan spirit, but rather to convince the unbelieving, such as solace themselves with the thought that all is well, while mischievous demagogues and fanatics are so earnestly forcing their counsels upon the chief national executive and his Cabinet for their guidance. A few extracts from leading newspapers will show what we mean. The *Washington Chronicle*, edited by Col. Forney, and often inspired by authority, says in plain words: "The extinction of slavery in the seceded States should be made a condition of their restoration to the Union."

The *Tribune* in nearly the same language says: "No member (of the Cabinet) barbors for a moment the idea of reconstructing the Union on a basis of slavery; and no flag of truce has been or will be entertained from disheartened rebel leaders which foreshadows any idea in conflict with the emancipation proclamation."

And the National Anti-Slavery *Standard*: "It is a great revolution in the midst of which we live. It is not an insurrection to be quelled and punished, and then all things to go on as before. It is a revolution which is to change the institutions of the nation and to give it a very different government from what it labored under before it began * * * For any final arrangement that shall leave slavery alive will amount to surrender at discretion."

All these organs, speaking in terms almost identical, and encouraged in these expressions by the achievements of our victorious armies, will carry home to the breasts of many reflecting men the conviction that no effort will be spared to drive the Administration into a straight-out anti-slavery war. There may yet be in the national capital too much enlightened patriotism to prevent such a deplorable consummation. Should such a policy succeed, however, none can foretell the years of war and desolation which are yet before us; some can estimate the blood and treasure to be wasted in this fratricidal strife. Nor is it certain that the free North, even to preserve for itself the form of civil government, could be held together for the prosecution of such a war. Indeed, the public safety depends on the overthrow and complete discomfiture of these visionary philosophers who, in the pursuit of Utopian ideas of universal emancipation by force of arms would spurn the thought of peace and reconstruction till the negro millennium so often described from the platforms of anti-slavery societies is ushered in.

Let us pray and labor that wiser counsels may prevail.--N.Y. Jour Commerce

THE SCRIPTURES AND THE DRAFT -- The following passage from the Scripture shows that in some cases, at least, its enforcement is opposed to the military regulations of the Children of Israel on the campaign through the wilderness: When a man hath taken a new wife, neither shalt he be charged with any new business, lest he shall be free at home one year and cheer up the wife he hath taken." The military laws and camp regulations of the army were otherwise very strict. No mention of a $300 exemption clause is made by the sacred tribe.

CAPT. JOHN FRAZIER, Provost Marshal for the eight Eastern Shore casualties of our State, arrived here from Easton on Wednesday last, and will return to his Headquarters tomorrow. The Captain's efficiency in the discharge of his duties and the becoming manner in which he performs them commends him to the favor of the people of this Shore as much as any one could be in such a position.

CAPT. G. W. P. Smith's Company of Independent Cavalry has been ordered to Eastville, Va., where it is supposed they will remain for some months. We are gratified to learn that Lt. Willis has fully recovered his health and returned to his duties.

The Trustees of Union Academy, in this town, on Wednesday last elected the Rev. John Fulton as Principle for the ensuing year. Rev. Geo. A. Phebus resigned and (Continued . . .)

Use this page to make notes about things you want to point out in the newspaper pages, things to compare and contrast with articles in today's papers, and/or to paste in a current front page for duplication.

Worcester County Shield

SNOW HILL, MD, SATURDAY MORNING, JULY 27, 1861

Worcester County Shield
Published every Saturday
by B. EVERETT SMITH

TERMS OF SUBSCRIPTION

TWO DOLLARS a year, invariably in arrears, to be paid within one month from the date of subscription. No papers will be given to any person except subscribers or advertisers.

THE LAW OF NEWSPAPERS

1. Subscribers who do not give express notice to the contrary are considered as wishing to continue their subscriptions.
2. If subscribers order the discontinuance of their papers, the publisher can continue to send them until arrears are paid.
3. If subscribers neglect or refuse to take their papers from the office to which they are directed, they are held responsible till they settle their bills, and order the paper discontinued.

THE DESPERATE CONFLICT BETWEEN "GRAND ARMY OF THE UNION" AND THE GRANDER ARMY OF JEFF DAVIS AT MANASSAS.

The repulse of the Federal Army near Manassas Junction, on Sunday last, through the effect of an absurd panic in one detachment of the Army, and which became general, after the most brilliant successes up to the very moment of retreat, resulted in the most serious disaster to General McDowell's army and to the prestige of the Union cause till then everywhere so triumphant. That it will be speedily repaired, no one at all conversant with the spirit and resources of the country will doubt. The details and incidents of the battle we give a large space to. It was fought, as it has since been publicly and unequivocally admitted by the President, and by Congressmen in the House, against the judgement of General Scott. Therefore it was massa Horace Greely, the "nigger worshipper's" generalship that suffers the disgrace, in which conviction there is much comfort; and we trust that hereafter Lieut. Gen. Scott will not read massa Greeley's Tribune, or any other abolition print, or allow editors to make plans of battle for him, or to suggest the time for action. In fact, he had better not read the papers at all, unless he is desirous of being continually convinced that he has a "fire in the rear." The disaster to the Federal arms in that important engagement was clearly the result of the impolicy of permitting civilian spectators within the lines--(a precaution the Confederates wisely pursued). --It is to them the panic on that part of the field where they were, and which became infectious, seems attributable. Also to inefficient and cowardly officers, to rashness and want of judgment--a thing to have expected--even with the brave. But if successes in almost every other battle attending the Union arms served as a punishment to those in rebellion against their Government, the reverses of the Federal arms before Manassas, just when victory was within grasp, of the inferior force of 40,000 to 90,000, strongly entrenched, and on the defensive, and who after so much more severely punishing the overwhelming numbers of the enemy in this greatest and most sanguinary conflict ever fought on this continent, will be felt by the abolitionists and other fools, fanatics, and desperadoes of the North, and in Congress as a deserved punishment to them at a dear cost to the Union cause. But to couple any other purpose with this war than the preservation of this Union, and consequently of a free government, in which alone can be enjoyed, "equal laws and equal rights" is to destroy these hopes at once. All designs or wishes opposed to the MORAL power engaged in maintaining the integrity of the Government, are dangerous and hateful. This presumption, stupidity, and wickedness of the Lovejoys, Wilsons, Greeleys, and others of them, who are at all times to be hated, have thus early been taught a most important lesson at the right time. Will they now learn how to properly appreciate the "Southern rebels?" Will they still consider them cowards and more braggarts, especially when commanded by such accomplished and experienced officers as Lee, Johnson, Beaureguard, and Davis? Whether in the next great engagement the Almighty will show to the rebellious army of the Confederates that He designs by turn to punish; if, indeed, they were not more severely punished than their retreated adversary,-- we shall wait to see. It may not be. Armies are but instruments of an unseen and inscrutable hand to punish man according to His infinite sense of justice. Neither does it follow that His punishment is to fall heaviest upon those with whom the greatest wrong, (in our finite judgement) exists.

Let us consider the position of Maryland and her interests in this dreadful and wicked struggle. Not being responsible for or in any way having sought to bring about this revolution, nor, again, having any sympathy with the abolition spirit so improperly, but very strongly intermixed with the necessarily defensive action of the Government under which we still exist, and shall ever hope to, except under circumstances worse than what we have yet suffered as originating in or by the Federal Government, our neutrality is the glory of our State, and it will, in any event, render her history classic as of this epoch. But for the circumstance of Virginia's unfortunate position in this war, and the sad necessity of the great battles of this revolution to be now fought upon her soil, we should long ere this have enrolled ourself in the army of the Union; but we have too many that are near and dear to us fighting there against the Union to render, it natural to desire to be in the way of their bullets, or that they--though wrong being yet sincere--run any risk from death-missles despatched by us even in the righteous cause of the Union. And what a horrible state of things is this. It is such considerations and feelings as these that influence the attitude of Union-loving Maryland. She will remain firm. And to her patriotic and sensible Governor are we mainly indebted for exemption from the horrors that are bing inflicted upon our late sister, Virginia. We invite attention to the Speech of Governor Hicks in Baltimore, to which we referred last week. What folly only and crime may yet accomplish to alter our present safe, honorable and happiest position, we cannot tell, but we have an abiding conviction that the people of Maryland are firmer than ever in their determination to maintain their neutrality. If Virginia soil should ever become distinguished for great victories over the Federal troops, it will be against the feelings and hopes of thousands of her own people, and there would be no results from them sufficient to compensate for the devastation that must mark the tracks of contending host. It is not her cause that is being fought out upon her soil, already drenched with the blood of a thousand of their own immediate brethren, if not more. She sought not this conflict, and it is waged against her moral sense. The fruits of it at best will be bitter, nor can ever compensate her people for their sacrifices. And while for no leader in this miserable, hell-begotten strife we can feel any sympathy, but desire to see them all confounded for what we believe to be their wicked and unscrupulous designs, we have a very different feeling for our misguided southern brethren in the ranks who are slain in this accursed war against our institutions and present form of Government, which we shall ever love and venerate. And again, when we bear in mind that the victors are often the greatest sufferers in killed and wounded, we cannot envy any one who can indulge in exultation at any slaughter that must ensue, while sitting indolently, and perhaps cowardly at home. God help the right. Amen.

THE NEWS

The accounts which we give elsewhere will explain fully as is now possible the reverse which overtook the Federal arms in front of Manassas Junction on Sunday evening. Up to four o'clock the fortunes of the day had been with the National forces. They had carried several batteries, but with great loss of life, and had exhibited a persistent courage that was thought would carry them persistently through. The position of the Confederates is represented to have been xxxxxxx [illegible on original document]. They were superior in numbers to their opponents, and behind a xxxxxxxxxx [illegible in original document]. As one of these was taken, it was found to be commanded or influenced by another. One of these batteries, so placed, it is reported was taken and lost seven times. The fighting at these points was stubborn, and the loss on both sides very heavy. finally the order was given to retreat; the retreat became a flight, and then grew into a panic, in which the troops rushed tummultuously toward Washington, many of them throwing away their arms, abandoning wagons, and losing a large portion of their artillery. On the origin of the panic different accounts ar given. The Confederates do not appear to have followed the retreating army very actively, and the loss on the road, except for one or two attacks, was not much. There were various reports at Washington on Sunday night in relation to the position of affairs. The men of the regiments attribute their disaster to bad generalship and are especially bitter towards Generals McDowell and Tyler and some of the regimental officers. At times it is stated that whole brigades were without proper leading and knew not where to look, or to whom for orders as to their xxxxxxxxxxx [illegible on original document]. A number of officers are among the killed and wounded.

The Government have met the emergency by ordering to Washington all the troops in camp in different States. McClellan has also been called from West Virginia to take command of the army. The force on the Virginia side of the Potomac has been increased by the despatch of several regiments thither, and those which suffered most severely in the battle brought into Washington for re-organization. General Banks, who has been transferred to the command of the force at Charlestown has proceeded to that point. Major General Dix takes command at Baltimore.

The United States Senate on Monday, voted, ayes 32, nays 6, the bill to confiscate property used for insurrectionary purposes, having first amended it, on motion of Mr. Trumnbil, by a provision declaring that "slaves employed in aiding in the rebellion against the Government, when captured shall be confiscated." The bill provides for the construction of one or more armored ships or batteries of ships passed.

GOVERNOR HICKS' SPEECH IN BALTIMORE

The following is the Speech of the governor of Maryland made in Baltimore on Tuesday night week upon the occasion of his being serenaded at the fountain Hotel, by the Blues Band, after his safe return from the Eastern Shore subsequent to the rumor of his assassination at Cambridge:--

The Governor appeared, he said, before the gentlemen of the Blues Band and the citizens of Baltimore to express his gratitude for the demonstrations of respect and kindness which had been extended him, and if he was not able to make a fine speech he would do the best he could. He was not a speech maker; that was not his vocation; but he was a working man, and he had the satisfaction of knowing that he was working in a good cause.

It was a great country in which he lived and he was proud of it, but he felt a greater degree of pride, still to think that it would remain a united country.

In this respect he would likeen it to the parents of a child, which, undergoing affliction, received even still more affection and kindness. Where, he exclaimed, "was the patriot who could fail to love and venerate the glorious Union, a Union which the blood of patriots had so dearly bought and paid for?" Although it was distorted and distracted, yet it still remained the admiration of every honest

WRITING ASSIGNMENT #3 - *Across Five Aprils*

PROMPT

"Be glad you're a boy, young feller, and don't hev to pester yourself with all these troubles that men be sufferin' through these days."

Pretend you are Jethro. Write a letter to the speaker of this statement persuading him that his statement is patronizing and untrue.

PREWRITING

Make a list of the things to which the speaker was referring. Next to each item, make a few notes explaining how it affects Jethro and/or why he is pestered by it.

Make a list of reasons why Jethro was exasperated by this statement.

DRAFTING

Begin in a letter format. Write a paragraph in which you introduce the topic you wish to discuss and make your main point that what the speaker said was patronizing and untrue.

Write one paragraph for each of the items to which the speaker was referring in his statement. Use a topic sentence in which you state the item to be discussed. Fill out your paragraph by explaining and using examples showing how the item being discussed does affect you (Jethro). Do this for each item.

Write a paragraph in which you conclude your letter, explaining why you were upset by his statement and making your final remarks.

PROMPT

When you finish the rough draft of your paper, ask a student who sits near you to read it. After reading your rough draft, he/she should tell you what he/she liked best about your work, which parts were difficult to understand, and ways in which your work could be improved. Reread your paper considering your critic's comments and make the corrections you think are necessary.

PROOFREADING

Do a final proofreading of your paper double-checking your grammar, spelling, organization, and the clarity of your ideas.

LESSON SIXTEEN

Objectives
1. To compare the Civil War era newspapers to today's newspapers
2. To show students that even today, different newspapers have different "slants" on issues
3. To familiarize students with the newspaper
4. To encourage students to read the newspaper

NOTE: Prior to this lesson you need to gather up three or four different newspapers for the same day. By doing this, you should be able to find the same stories covered but written with different slants, depending on the philosophies of the reporters and editors for each story.

Make transparencies of the stories you wish to compare if the newspapers won't give you class sets of each.

Activity
Read through the front page articles (or the articles you are comparing) with students. Show students (or ask them) how each article relates the same information but in slightly different ways.

Discuss the various parts of the newspaper. Compare the kinds of things in our newspapers today with the kinds of things in the Civil War era newspapers.

The newspapers from the Civil War era were a total of about 4 to 8 pages, for the most part. Today's papers are much larger. Discuss the impact of technology on the printing of newspapers.

LESSON SEVENTEEN

Objective
To review the main ideas presented in *Across Five Aprils*

Activity #1
Choose one of the review games/activities included in this guide and spend your class period as outlined there. Some materials for these activities are located in the Extra Activities section of this unit.

Activity #2
Remind students that the Unit Test will be in the next class meeting. Stress the review of the Study Guides and their class notes as a last-minute, brush-up review for homework.

REVIEW GAMES/ACTIVITIES - *Across Five Aprils*

1. Ask the class to make up a unit test for *Across Five Aprils*. The test should have 4 sections: matching, true/false, short answer, and essay. Students may use 1/2 period to make the test and then swap papers and use the other 1/2 class period to take a test a classmate has devised. (open book) You may want to use the unit test included in this guide or take questions from the students' unit tests to formulate your own test.

2. Take 1/2 period for students to make up true and false questions (including the answers). Collect the papers and divide the class into two teams. Draw a big tic-tac-toe board on the chalk board. Make one team X and one team O. Ask questions to each side, giving each student one turn. If the question is answered correctly, that students' team's letter (X or O) is placed in the box. If the answer is incorrect, no mark is placed in the box. The object is to get three marks in a row like tic-tac-toe. You may want to keep track of the number of games won for each team.

3. Take 1/2 period for students to make up questions (true/false and short answer). Collect the questions. Divide the class into two teams. You'll alternate asking questions to individual members of teams A & B (like in a spelling bee). The question keeps going from A to B until it is correctly answered, then a new question is asked. A correct answer does not allow the team to get another question. Correct answers are +2 points; incorrect answers are -1 point.

4. Have students pair up and quiz each other from their study guides and class notes.

5. Give students a *Across Five Aprils* crossword puzzle to complete.

6. Divide your class into two teams. Use the *Across Five Aprils* crossword words with their letters jumbled as a word list. Student 1 from Team A faces off against Student 1 from Team B. You write the first jumbled word on the board. The first student (1A or 1B) to unscramble the word wins the chance for his/her team to score points. If 1A wins the jumble, go to student 2A and give him/her a clue. He/she must give you the correct word which matches that clue. If he/she does, Team A scores a point, and you give student 3A a clue for which you expect another correct response. Continue giving Team A clues until some team member makes an incorrect response. An incorrect response sends the game back to the jumbled-word face off, this time with students 2A and 2B. Instead of repeating giving clues to the first few students of each team, continue with the student after the one who gave the last incorrect response on the team. For example, if Team B wins the jumbled-word face-off, and student 5B gave the last incorrect answer for Team B, you would start this round of clue questions with student 6B, and so on. The team with the most points wins!

LESSON TWENTY

Objective
To test the students' understanding of the main ideas and themes in *Across Five Aprils*

Activity #1
Distribute the unit tests. Go over the instructions in detail and allow the students the entire class period to complete the exam.

NOTES ABOUT THE UNIT TESTS IN THIS UNIT:
There are 5 different unit tests which follow.

There are two short answer tests which are based primarily on facts from the novel.

There is one advanced short answer unit test. It is based on the extra discussion questions and quotations. Use the matching key for short answer unit test 2 to check the matching section of the advanced short answer unit test. There is no key for the short answer questions and quotations. The answers will be based on the discussions you have had during class.

There are two multiple choice unit tests. Following the two unit tests, you will find an answer sheet on which students should mark their answers. The same answer sheet should be used for both tests; however, students' answers will be different for each test. Following the students' answer sheet for the multiple choice tests you will find your answer keys.

The short answer tests have a vocabulary section. You should choose 10 of the vocabulary words from this unit, read them orally and have the students write them down. Then, either have students write a definition or use the words in sentences.

Use these words for the vocabulary section of the advanced short answer unit test:

abolitionists	amiable	apathy	contemptuous
dissipated	incoherent	inept	ominous
preponderance	reiterated	tenacity	wanly

Activity #2
Collect all test papers and assigned books prior to the end of the class period.

UNIT TESTS

SHORT ANSWER UNIT TEST 1 - *Across Five Aprils*

I. Matching/Identify

___ 1. Ellen   A. President

___ 2. Bill   B. Editor

___ 3. Lincoln   C. Ellen's nephew

___ 4. Jethro   D. Teacher

___ 5. Grant   E. Rode with Jethro through danger & saved him

___ 6. Wortman   F. Marries Shad Yale

___ 7. Milton   G. Died on the battlefield

___ 8. John   H. Southern general

___ 9. Shadrach   I. Jethro's mother

___ 10. Wilse   J. Killed in an accident

___ 11. Mary   K. Wanted Jethro to bring him a newspaper

___ 12. Dave Burdow   L. Mob leader who threatened Jethro

___ 13. Lee   M. John's wife

___ 14. Eb   N. Brings news of Tom's death

___ 15. Tom   O. Northern general

___ 16. Matt   P. Jethro wrote to Lincoln about his desertion

___ 17. Jenny   Q. Young boy who grew up during the Civil War

___ 18. Dan Lawrence   R. Bill and he were close brothers who had a fight

___ 19. Nancy   S. Jethro's father

___ 20. Jake Roscoe   T. Went to fight for the South

Across Five Aprils Short Answer Unit Test Page 2

II. Short Answer

1. What kinds of things were troubling the adult world on that first April morning?

2. How did Tom and Eb feel about the prospects of war?

3. What had happened to Jethro's sister, Mary?

4. What effect did the Confederate victories at Bull Run and Ball's Bluff have on the Northerners?

5. Why did Bill have to leave?

6. How did Shad make Jethro understand the war?

7. What trouble did Jethro have in Newton?

8. What happened to Jethro and Dave Burdow by the bridge?

Across Five Aprils Short Answer Unit Test 1 Page 3

9. Why did Jethro say he had left childhood behind him in that March of 1862?

10. What was the feeling of the community towards the Creightons?

11. How did Guy Wortman get what was coming to him?

12. Why was the Union army demoralized in 1862?

13. Why did the Federal Registrars visit the Creightons' farm?

14. From whom did Jethro get an important letter, and what did it say?

15. Why did Jenny go to Washington?

16. What were Ross Milton's thoughts about the thirteenth amendment?

17. How did Jethro feel about Lincoln's death?

Across Five Aprils Short Answer Unit Test 1 Page 4

III. Composition

What is the point of *Across Five Aprils*? When we read books, we usually come away from our reading experience a little richer, having given more thought to a particular aspect of life. What do you think Irene Hunt intended us to gain from reading her novel?

Across Five Aprils Short Answer Unit Test 1 Page 5

IV. Vocabulary
   Listen to the vocabulary words and write them down.
   Go back later and fill in the correct definition for each word.

1.

2.

3.

4.

5.

6.

7.

8.

9.

10.

SHORT ANSWER UNIT TEST 2 - *Across Five Aprils*

I. Matching

___ 1. Ellen   A. Marries Shad Yale

___ 2. Bill   B. Killed in an accident

___ 3. Lincoln   C. Wanted Jethro to bring him a newspaper

___ 4. Jethro   D. John's wife

___ 5. Grant   E. Teacher

___ 6. Wortman   F. President

___ 7. Milton   G. Died on the battlefield

___ 8. John   H. Brings news of Tom's death

___ 9. Shadrach   I. Jethro's mother

___ 10. Wilse   J. Editor

___ 11. Mary   K. Northern general

___ 12. Dave Burdow   L. Mob leader who threatened Jethro

___ 13. Lee   M. Rode with Jethro through danger & saved him

___ 14. Eb   N. Southern general

___ 15. Tom   O. Ellen's nephew

___ 16. Matt   P. Young boy who grew up during the Civil War

___ 17. Jenny   Q. Jethro wrote to Lincoln about his desertion

___ 18. Dan Lawrence   R. Jethro's father

___ 19. Nancy   S. Bill and he were close brothers who had a fight

___ 20. Jake Roscoe   T. Went to fight for the South

Across Five Aprils Short Answer Unit Test 2 Page 2

II. Short Answer

1. Why did Jethro say he had left childhood behind him in that March of 1862?

2. What was the feeling of the community towards the Creightons?

3. Why was the Union army demoralized in 1862?

4. How did Jethro feel about harboring Eb?

5. How did Jethro feel about Lincoln's death?

Across Five Aprils Short Answer Unit Test 2 Page 3

III. Composition

1. Describe the relationship between:

   Jethro and Bill

   Jethro and John

   Jethro and Shad

   Jethro and Jenny

Across Five Aprils Short Answer Unit Test 2 Page 4

2. Explain how *Across Five Aprils* is a story about growing up and growing older.

3. What are the conflicts in the story and how are they resolved?

Across Five Aprils Short Answer Unit Test 2 Page 5

4. Explain how Irene Hunt uses *Across Five Aprils* to show the effect of the Civil War on a personal level.

5. List at least five things you learned about the American Civil War while studying *Across Five Aprils*.

Across Five Aprils Short Answer Unit Test 2 Page 5

IV. Vocabulary
   Listen to the vocabulary words and write them down.
   Go back later and fill in the correct definition for each word.

1.

2.

3.

4.

5.

6.

7.

8.

9.

10.

KEY: SHORT ANSWER UNIT TESTS - *Across Five Aprils*

The short answer questions are taken directly from the study guides.
If you need to look up the answers, you will find them in the study guide section.

Answers to the composition questions will vary depending on your
class discussions and the level of your students.

For the vocabulary section of the test, choose ten of the
words from the vocabulary lists to read orally for your students.

The answers to the matching section of the test are below.

Answers to the matching section of the Advanced Short Answer Unit Test
are the same as for Short Answer Unit Test #2.

Test #1	Test #2
1. I	1. I
2. R	2. T
3. A	3. F
4. Q	4. P
5. O	5. K
6. L	6. L
7. B	7. J
8. R	8. S
9. D	9. E
10. C	10. O
11. J	11. B
12. E	12. M
13. H	13. N
14. P	14. Q
15. G	15. G
16. S	16. R
17. F	17. A
18. N	18. H
19. M	19. D
20. K	20. C

ADVANCED SHORT ANSWER UNIT TEST - *Across Five Aprils*

I. Matching

___ 1. Ellen   A. Marries Shad Yale

___ 2. Bill   B. Killed in an accident

___ 3. Lincoln   C. Wanted Jethro to bring him a newspaper

___ 4. Jethro   D. John's wife

___ 5. Grant   E. Teacher

___ 6. Wortman   F. President

___ 7. Milton   G. Died on the battlefield

___ 8. John   H. Brings news of Tom's death

___ 9. Shadrach   I. Jethro's mother

___ 10. Wilse   J. Editor

___ 11. Mary   K. Northern general

___ 12. Dave Burdow   L. Mob leader who threatened Jethro

___ 13. Lee   M. Rode with Jethro through danger & saved him

___ 14. Eb   N. Southern general

___ 15. Tom   O. Ellen's nephew

___ 16. Matt   P. Young boy who grew up during the Civil War

___ 17. Jenny   Q. Jethro wrote to Lincoln about his desertion

___ 18. Dan Lawrence   R. Jethro's father

___ 19. Nancy   S. Bill and he were close brothers who had a fight

___ 20. Jake Roscoe   T. Went to fight for the South

Across Five Aprils Advanced Short Answer Unit Test Page 2
II. Short Answer
1. Choose any three of the minor characters in the story and explain how each was important.

    A.

    B.

    C.

2. Give at least two examples of foreshadowing used in *Across Five Aprils*.

3. Explain the use of darkness, night, and nightmares in *Across Five Aprils*.

4. Give at least two examples of the romantic view of war versus the realistic view of war in *Across Five Aprils*.

Across Five Aprils Advanced Short Answer Unit Test Page 3

5. How is education important as a theme in *Across Five Aprils*?

6. Explain how *Across Five Aprils* shows how the Civil War affected family unity, particularly in the "border states."

7. Explain how the title of the book is appropriate.

Across Five Aprils Advanced Short Answer Unit Test Page 4

III. Composition

The *Chicago Tribune* said, "This is a beautifully written book, filled with bloodshed, hate, and tears, but also with love, loyalty, and compassion with unforgettable characters, and with ideas and implications that have meaning for young people today."

Defend this statement using specific examples from the text.

Across Five Aprils Advanced Short Answer Unit Test Page 5

III. Vocabulary

    Write down the vocabulary words you are given. Go back later and use all of those vocabulary words in a composition relating to *Across Five Aprils*.

MULTIPLE CHOICE UNIT TEST 1 - *Across Five Aprils*

I. Matching/Identify

___ 1. Ellen   A. President

___ 2. Bill   B. Editor

___ 3. Lincoln   C. Ellen's nephew

___ 4. Jethro   D. Teacher

___ 5. Grant   E. Rode with Jethro through danger & saved him

___ 6. Wortman   F. Marries Shad Yale

___ 7. Milton   G. Died on the battlefield

___ 8. John   H. Southern general

___ 9. Shadrach   I. Jethro's mother

___ 10. Wilse   J. Killed in an accident

___ 11. Mary   K. Wanted Jethro to bring him a newspaper

___ 12. Dave Burdow   L. Mob leader who threatened Jethro

___ 13. Lee   M. John's wife

___ 14. Eb   N. Brings news of Tom's death

___ 15. Tom   O. Northern general

___ 16. Matt   P. Jethro wrote to Lincoln about his desertion

___ 17. Jenny   Q. Young boy who grew up during the Civil War

___ 18. Dan Lawrence   R. Bill and he were close brothers who had a fight

___ 19. Nancy   S. Jethro's father

___ 20. Jake Roscoe   T. Went to fight for the South

Across Five Aprils Multiple Choice Unit Test 1 Page 2

II. Multiple Choice

1. Which of the following was not troubling the adult world on that first April morning?
    A. Cinchbugs and grasshoppers
    B. Drought
    C. Secession and talk of war
    D. Inflation

2. How did Jethro's feelings towards war change after listening to the conversation among the men?
    A. He became troubled and feared what war would bring.
    B. He was excited at the glorious prospects of fighting.
    C. He became sad at the prospects of so many deaths.
    D. He wished he lived in the North.

3. Why was Jenny upset about the war?
    A. She couldn't get any fabric to make new dresses or quilts.
    B. Shad would be going off to war before her father would allow her to marry him.
    C. She wanted to fight, and women were not permitted to join the service.
    D. She was afraid it would come to their area and they would all be killed.

4. What trouble did Jethro have in Newton?
    A. He didn't know how to park the wagon.
    B. He got lost and couldn't find the store.
    C. Some men harassed him because Bill had gone to fight with the Rebs.
    D. He didn't have enough money to pay for everything he bought. The shopkeeper thought Jethro was trying to cheat him.

5. What happened by the bridge?
    A. The bridge collapsed.
    B. Jethro found a dead body with a Confederate flag draped over it.
    C. A snake scared the horses, and Jethro had to fight to keep control of them.
    D. Someone tried to attack the wagon and scare the horses. Dave Burdow saved Jethro by holding the team steady.

6. What happened in March of 1862?
    A. Jethro inherited a large sum of money.
    B. Jethro went away to college.
    C. Jethro became the man of the house and left his childhood behind him.
    D. Jethro was old enough to enlist in the army.

Across Five Aprils Multiple Choice Unit Test 1 Page 3

7. How did the community show support for Matt Creighton that spring?
    A. They paid his mortgage.
    B. The men took turns driving him to the doctor in the next town.
    C. They donated grain and equipment and worked his fields.
    D. They held a "Matt Creighton Appreciation Day" service at church.

8. What kind of letter did Ross Milton put into his paper?
    A. He said the Creightons had suffered enough by the sacrifices their sons had made and asked the night vandals what they had done for the Union.
    B. He offered a substantial reward for any information about the identification of the vandals.
    C. He called for the town to unite and have a Union Support Day where they all made bandages and wrote letters to the soldiers.
    D. He prayed for a quick end to the war.

9. What did the men think of General Mc Clellan?
    A. They thought he was a braggart and a fool who would never win the war.
    B. They thought he was marginal but was the best possible choice.
    C. They wholeheartedly supported him.
    D. Their opinions were split, which was also causing dissention among the troops.

10. Who was Ambrose Burnside?
    A. He was a famous newspaper reporter who chronicled the war in great detail.
    B. He was the military strategic advisor to the President.
    C. He was a Union general who sent thousands of soldiers to their deaths in the hills of Virginia.
    D. He was a doctor who developed new treatments for treating wounded soldiers right on the battlefield.

11. What was going on at Point Prospect?
    A. There was a prisoner of war camp.
    B. There was a field hospital that was treating wounded from both sides.
    C. A group of pacifists were organizing to march on Washington.
    D. Deserters were camping there, terrorizing the neighborhood.

Across Five Aprils Multiple Choice Unit Test 1 Page 4

12. Why did the Federal Registrars visit the Creightons' farm?
    A. They were looking for Eb, who had deserted.
    B. They were looking for more boys to enlist. Someone had told them that Jethro was old enough to go.
    C. They were looking for a place to set up a spying operation and wanted to use the Creighton farm.
    D. Matt Creighton owed back taxes, and they were there to collect.

13. What did Jenny think was bothering Jethro?
    A. She thought he had been smoking and had made himself sick.
    B. She thought he was in love.
    C. She thought it was just puberty.
    D. She thought he was too preoccupied with thoughts of the war.

14. What did Eb do?
    A. He rejoined the army, dug ditches, and endured the scorn of the other soldiers.
    B. He ran away and joined the army of the South.
    C. He killed himself.
    D. He took on a new identity and moved West.

15. What were people's feelings about the battle at Gettysburg?
    A. They saw it as the turning point of the war.
    B. Most thought too many lives had been lost.
    C. They were glad for the victory but puzzled that the Union had given up the opportunity to crush Lee's army.
    D. They didn't think it was a very significant battle because it had been fought in the North. They thought the really important battles were fought in the South.

16. What did Shad think of General Grant?
    A. He had confidence that this man would win the war for the North.
    B He thought Grant was just another in a long line of poor generals.
    C. He reminded him of his uncle.
    D. He thought he was a wimp.

17. What were Ross Milton's thoughts about peace?
    A. An end to the war would create an immediate peace.
    B. There would never be peace as long as people still secretly supported the South.
    C. Men were not naturally peaceful creatures, and it wouldn't last. They would start another war somewhere else.
    D. Peace would be hard to come by, and the scars from the war would be a long time in healing.

III. Composition

    ALA Booklist said, ". . . Drawing from family records and from stories told by her grandfather, the author has, in an uncommonly fine narrative, created living characters and vividly reconstructed a crucial period of history."

    Using examples from the book *Across Five Aprils*, defend this statement.

Across Five Aprils Multiple Choice Unit Test 1 Page 6

IV. Vocabulary   Match the correct definitions to the words.

___ 1. Agonizingly   a. desperate outlaw

___ 2. Belligerently   b. with great pain or difficulty

___ 3. Permeating   c. one who wastes things

___ 4. Tyrannical   d. scornful

___ 5. Passel   e. holding or sticking to something persistently

___ 6. Tenacity   f. a bunch; many

___ 7. Bunting   g. shrewd; smart concerning one's own affairs

___ 8. Loathing   h. kindly; pleasantly

___ 9. Astute   i. reprimands

___ 10. Desperado   j. threatening

___ 11. Apathy   k. penetrating; spreading throughout

___ 12. Admonitions   l. defiantly; in a hostile manner

___ 13. Contemptuous   m. indifference

___ 14. Pandemonium   n. feeling of repulsion

___ 15. Ominous   o. majority

___ 16. Genially   p. deliberately avoided

___ 17. Preponderance   q. oppressively domineering

___ 18. Wastrel   r. believability

___ 19. Shunned   s. wild uproar

___ 20. Credence   t. strips of material in patriotic colors used for festive decorations

MULTIPLE CHOICE UNIT TEST 2 - *Across Five Aprils*

I. Matching

1. Ellen
2. Bill
3. Lincoln
4. Jethro
5. Grant
6. Wortman
7. Milton
8. John
9. Shadrach
10. Wilse
11. Mary
12. Dave Burdow
13. Lee
14. Eb
15. Tom
16. Matt
17. Jenny
18. Dan Lawrence
19. Nancy
20. Jake Roscoe

A. Marries Shad Yale
B. Killed in an accident
C. Wanted Jethro to bring him a newspaper
D. John's wife
E. Teacher
F. President
G. Died on the battlefield
H. Brings news of Tom's death
I. Jethro's mother
J. Editor
K. Northern general
L. Mob leader who threatened Jethro
M. Rode with Jethro through danger & saved him
N. Southern general
O. Ellen's nephew
P. Young boy who grew up during the Civil War
Q. Jethro wrote to Lincoln about his desertion
R. Jethro's father
S. Bill and he were close brothers who had a fight
T. Went to fight for the South

Across Five Aprils Multiple Choice Unit Test 2 Page 2

II. Multiple Choice

1. Which of the following was not troubling the adult world on that first April morning?
    A. Cinchbugs and grasshoppers
    B. Inflation
    C. Secession and talk of war
    D. Drought

2. How did Jethro's feelings towards war change after hearing the conversation among the men?
    A. He was excited at the glorious prospects of fighting.
    B. He became troubled and feared what war would bring.
    C. He became sad at the prospects of so many deaths.
    D. He wished he lived in the North.

3. Why was Jenny upset about the war?
    A. She couldn't get any fabric to make new dresses or quilts.
    B. She wanted to fight, and women were not permitted to join the service.
    C. Shad would be going off to war before her father would allow her to marry him.
    D. She was afraid it would come to their area and they would all be killed.

4. What trouble did Jethro have in Newton?
    A. He didn't know how to park the wagon.
    B. He got lost and couldn't find the store.
    C. He didn't have enough money to pay for everything he bought. The shopkeeper thought Jethro was trying to cheat him.
    D. Some men harassed him because Bill had gone to fight with the Rebs.

5. What happened by the bridge?
    A. Someone tried to attack the wagon and scare the horses. Dave Burdow saved Jethro by holding the team steady.
    B. Jethro found a dead body with a Confederate flag draped over it.
    C. A snake scared the horses, and Jethro had to fight to keep control of them.
    D. The bridge collapsed.

6. What happened in March of 1862?
    A. Jethro inherited a large sum of money.
    B. Jethro became the man of the house and left his childhood behind him.
    C. Jethro went away to college.
    D. Jethro was old enough to enlist in the army.

Across Five Aprils Multiple Choice Unit Test 2 Page 3

7. How did the community show support for Matt Creighton that spring?
   A. They paid his mortgage.
   B. The men took turns driving him to the doctor in the next town.
   C. They held a "Matt Creighton Appreciation Day" service at church.
   D. They donated grain and equipment and worked his fields.

8. What kind of letter did Ross Milton put into his paper?
   A. He prayed for a quick end to the war.
   B. He offered a substantial reward for any information about the identification of the vandals.
   C. He called for the town to unite and have a Union Support Day where they all made bandages and wrote letters to the soldiers.
   D. He said the Creightons had suffered enough by the sacrifices their sons had made and asked the night vandals what they had done for the Union.

9. What did the men think of General McClellan?
   A. They wholeheartedly supported him.
   B. They thought he was marginal but was the best possible choice.
   C. They thought he was a braggart and a fool, who would never win the war.
   D. Their opinions were split, which was also causing dissention among the troops.

10. Who was Ambrose Burnside?
    A. He was a famous newspaper reporter who chronicled the war in great detail.
    B. He was a Union general who sent thousands of soldiers to their deaths in the hills of Virginia.
    C. He was the military strategic advisor to the President.
    D. He was a doctor who developed new treatments for treating wounded soldiers right on the battlefield.

11. What was going on at Point Prospect?
    A. There was a prisoner of war camp.
    B. There was a field hospital that was treating wounded from both sides.
    C. Deserters were camping there, terrorizing the neighborhood.
    D. A group of pacifists were organizing to march on Washington.

Across Five Aprils Multiple Choice Unit Test 2 Page 4

12. Why did the Federal Registrars visit the Creightons' farm?
    A. They were looking for more boys to enlist. Someone had told them that Jethro was old enough to go.
    B. They were looking for Eb, who had deserted.
    C. They were looking for a place to set up a spying operation and wanted to use the Creighton farm.
    D. Matt Creighton owed back taxes, and they were there to collect.

13. What did Jenny think was bothering Jethro?
    A. She thought it was just puberty.
    B. She thought he was in love.
    C. She thought he had been smoking and had made himself sick.
    D. She thought he was too preoccupied with thoughts of the war.

14. What did Eb do?
    A. He killed himself.
    B. He ran away and joined the army of the South.
    C. He rejoined the army, dug ditches, and endured the scorn of the other soldiers.
    D. He took on a new identity and moved West.

15. What were people's feelings about the battle at Gettysburg?
    A. They didn't think it was a very significant battle because it had been fought in the North. They thought the really important battles were fought in the South.
    B. Most thought too many lives had been lost.
    C. They were glad for the victory but puzzled that the Union had given up the opportunity to crush Lee's army.
    D. They saw it as the turning point of the war.

16. What did Shad think of General Grant?
    A. He thought Grant was just another in a long line of poor generals.
    B He had confidence that this man would win the war for the North.
    C. He reminded him of his uncle.
    D. He thought he was a wimp.

17. What were Ross Milton's thoughts about peace?
    A. Peace would be hard to come by and the scars from the war would be a long time in healing.
    B. There would never be peace as long as people still secretly supported the South.
    C. Men were not naturally peaceful creatures, and it wouldn't last. They would start another war somewhere else.
    D. An end to the war would create an immediate peace.

Across Five Aprils Multiple Choice Unit Test 2 Page 5

III. Composition

    The University of Chicago Center for Children's Books said, "An impressive book both as a historically authenticated Civil War novel and as a beautifully written family story. . . . The realistic treatment of the intricate emotional conflicts within a border state family is superb. The details of battles and campaigns are deftly integrated into letters and conversations, and the characters are completely convincing."

Using specific examples from the book, support and defend this statement.

Across Five Aprils Multiple Choice Unit Test 2 Page 6

IV. Vocabulary   Match the correct definitions to the words.

___ 1. Admonitions   a. kindly; pleasantly

___ 2. Inept   b. strips of material in patriotic colors used for festive decorations

___ 3. Mammoth   c. scornful

___ 4. Shunned   d. huge

___ 5. Gaiety   e. tolerated

___ 6. Dissipated   f. to shelter

___ 7. Brooked   g. a bunch; many

___ 8. Bunting   h. Something that engrosses the mind

___ 9. Belligerently   i. in a way showing one tired or sad

___ 10. Preoccupation   j. festivity; happiness

___ 11. Tenacity   k. fixed; corrected

___ 12. Wanly   l. defiantly; in a hostile manner

___ 13. Passel   m. dispersed; sent or went away

___ 14. Pandemonium   n. incompetent

___ 15. Harbor   o. revengefulness

___ 16. Contemptuous   p. reprimands

___ 17. Genially   q. deliberately avoided

___ 18. Vindictiveness   r. 19th century war ships having sides with metal plates as armor

___ 19. Ironclads   s. holding or sticking to something persistently

___ 20. Amended   t. wild uproar

ANSWER SHEET - *Across Five Aprils*
Multiple Choice Unit Tests

I. Matching	II. Multiple Choice	IV. Vocabulary
1. ___	1. ___	1. ___
2. ___	2. ___	2. ___
3. ___	3. ___	3. ___
4. ___	4. ___	4. ___
5. ___	5. ___	5. ___
6. ___	6. ___	6. ___
7. ___	7. ___	7. ___
8. ___	8. ___	8. ___
9. ___	9. ___	9. ___
10. ___	10. ___	10. ___
11. ___	11. ___	11. ___
12. ___	12. ___	12. ___
13. ___	13. ___	13. ___
14. ___	14. ___	14. ___
15. ___	15. ___	15. ___
16. ___	16. ___	16. ___
17. ___	17. ___	17. ___
18. ___		18. ___
19. ___		19. ___
20. ___		20. ___

ANSWER KEY MULTIPLE CHOICE UNIT TESTS – *Across Five Aprils*

Answers to Unit Test 1 are in the left column. Answers to Unit Test 2 are in the right column.

I. Matching		II. Multiple Choice		IV. Vocabulary	
1. I	I	1. D	B	1. B	P
2. T	T	2. A	B	2. L	N
3. A	F	3. B	C	3. K	D
4. Q	P	4. C	D	4. Q	Q
5. O	K	5. D	A	5. F	J
6. L	L	6. C	B	6. E	M
7. B	J	7. C	D	7. T	E
8. R	S	8. A	D	8. N	B
9. D	E	9. A	C	9. G	L
10. C	O	10. C	B	10. A	H
11. J	B	11. D	C	11. M	S
12. E	M	12. A	B	12. I	I
13. H	N	13. A	C	13. D	G
14. P	Q	14. A	C	14. S	T
15. G	G	15. A	D	15. J	F
16. S	R	16. A	B	16. H	C
17. F	A	17. D	A	17. O	A
18. N	H			18. C	O
19. M	D			19. P	R
20. K	C			20. R	K

UNIT RESOURCE MATERIALS

BULLETIN BOARD IDEAS - *Across Five Aprils*

1. Save one corner of the board for the best of students' *Across Five Aprils* writing assignments.

2. Take one of the word search puzzles from the extra activities section and with a marker copy it over in a large size on the bulletin board. Write the clue words to find to one side. Invite students prior to and after class to find the words and circle them on the bulletin board.

3. Write several of the most significant quotations from the book on the board on brightly colored paper.

4. Make a bulletin board listing the vocabulary words for this unit. As you complete sections of the novel and discuss the vocabulary for each section, write the definitions on the bulletin board. (If your board is one students face frequently, it will help them learn the words.)

5. Post copies of newspaper articles about the Civil War from your local archives.

6. Post copies of the front page articles of your daily newspaper for students to read. (Post the entire front page and clips from other pages on which articles from the front page have been continued.)

7. Post the map group's map on the bulletin board for reference during the unit.

8. Post letters to the editor from your local newspaper.

9. Post pictures of Civil War battles from your library's picture file. Or purchase a book about the Civil War with lots of pictures in it, cut out, and laminate the pictures to post. You can use these year after year.

10. Do a bulletin board about the history of civil rights, beginning with the Civil War.

11. Do a bulletin board about military careers and/or careers in agriculture.

12. Post photos of the people mentioned in the book: Lincoln, Grant, Lee, Burnside, McClellan, etc.

13. Prepare the bulletin board with the title, "ACROSS FIVE APRILS: A CIVIL WAR NOVEL" and blank background paper. As an introductory activity, have each student go to the board and, using a marker, write one fact he/she knows about the Civil War. Go around the room as many times as possible until your board is filled with Civil War facts. Use lots of different colored markers.

EXTRA ACTIVITIES – *Across Five Aprils*

One of the difficulties in teaching a novel is that all students don't read at the same speed. One student who likes to read may take the book home and finish it in a day or two. Sometimes a few students finish the in-class assignments early. The problem, then, is finding suitable extra activities for students.

The best thing I've found is to keep a little library in the classroom. For this unit on *Across Five Aprils,* you might check out from the school library other related books and articles about the Civil War, journalism, "growing up," military careers, war, death and emotionally dealing with death, the family unit and family relationships, medicine at the time of the Civil War, etc. Keeping local newspapers on hand is a good idea, too. Articles about the author, criticisms of her works, or other books by the author would also be appropriate.

Other things you may keep on hand are puzzles. We have made some relating directly to *Across Five Aprils* for you. Feel free to duplicate them.

Some students may like to draw. You might devise a contest or allow some extra-credit grade for students who draw characters or scenes from *Across Five Aprils*. Note, too, that if the students do not want to keep their drawings you may pick up some extra bulletin board materials this way. If you have a contest and you supply the prize (a CD or something like that perhaps), you could, possibly, make the drawing itself a non-refundable entry fee.

The pages which follow contain games, puzzles and worksheets. The keys, when appropriate, immediately follow the puzzle or worksheet. There are two main groups of activities: one group for the unit; that is, generally relating to the *Across Five Aprils* text, and another group of activities related strictly to the vocabulary.

Directions for these games, puzzles and worksheets are self-explanatory. The object here is to provide you with extra materials you may use in any way you choose.

MORE ACTIVITIES - *Across Five Aprils*

1. Pick a chapter or scene with a great deal of dialogue and have the students act it out on a stage. (Perhaps you could assign various scenes to different groups of students so more than one scene could be acted and more students could participate.)

2. Use some of the related topics (noted earlier for an in-class library) as topics for research, reports, or as topics for guest speakers.

3. Have students design a book cover (front and back and inside flaps) for *Across Five Aprils*.

4. Have students design a bulletin board (ready to be put up; not just sketched) for *Across Five Aprils*.

5. If your school is close to a Civil War battlefield, take a class trip to explore it.

6. Have students create a Civil War board game for *Across Five Aprils* in which they use the characters, settings, and events from the novel.

7. Follow this unit with a mini-unit on grammar using the text of *Across Five Aprils* as the source for the sentences you study.

8. Divide your class into pairs. Each pair of students should pick one historical figure from the Civil War era and study that person in depth. Together the students should prepare an interview of that character to perform in front of the class. One student should be the interviewer and the other student should be the historical figure being interviewed. Having students dress in costumes would be fun.

9. Have students write one of the following letters:
    a. A letter from Jethro to Dave Burdow after the incident at the bridge
    b. A letter from Eb to President Lincoln after his "pardon"
    c. A letter from Tom to Jethro about the realities of war
    d. A letter from Ellen to Shad about Jethro

Across Five Aprils Word List

No.	Word	Clue/Definition
1.	ADULTS	They were troubled by drought, elections, slavery, secession & talk of war
2.	AMENDMENT	The 13th ____ freed slaves
3.	APPOMATTOX	Courthouse where the South surrendered
4.	BARN	People set the Creighton's on fire
5.	BILL	Went to fight for the South
6.	BLUFF	Ball's ____
7.	BRIDGE	Place where Jethro & Dave Burdow were attacked
8.	BULL	____ Run
9.	CHILDHOOD	Jethro left his behind him in March 1862
10.	CONFEDERATES	Fighters for the South
11.	DAN	Lawrence; Brings news of Tom's death
12.	DANCE	Where Mary had been the night she was killed
13.	DAVE	Burdow who rode with Jethro & saved him
14.	DESERTER	What Eb became by leaving the army
15.	DITCHES	Eb's job was digging these when he rejoined the army
16.	EB	Jethro wrote to Lincoln about his desertion
17.	ELLEN	Jethro's mother
18.	GRANT	Northern general
19.	HENRY	The union began to win after the fall of Fort ____ in Tennessee
20.	JENNY	Married Shad Yale
21.	JETHRO	Young boy who grew up during the Civil War
22.	JOHN	Bill & he were close brothers who had a fight
23.	LEE	Southern general
24.	LINCOLN	President during the Civil War
25.	MANHOOD	Jethro's going to town alone was a step towards his ____.
26.	MARY	Was killed in an accident
27.	MATT	Jethro's father
28.	MILTON	Editor
29.	NANCY	John's wife
30.	PROSPECT	Point ____; deserters' camp
31.	READ	Ellen gave the letter to Jethro because she could not ____.
32.	ROSCOE	Jake; wanted Jethro to bring him a newspaper
33.	SAVANNAH	Sherman's gift to Lincoln
34.	SCARED	Bill told Jethro that being ____ was nothing to be ashamed of
35.	SHADRACH	Teacher
36.	SHILOH	Jethro considered the victory here to be empty like Pittsburgh landing
37.	SUMTER	Confederates fired on this fort and the war started
38.	TOM	Died on the battlefield
39.	TURKEY	Call Eb used in the woods
40.	WASHINGTON	Jenny went there to see Shad
41.	WILSE	Ellen's nephew
42.	WILSON	____'s Creek; battle close to Creighton's home; Union lost
43.	WORTMAN	Mob leader who threatened Jethro

WORD SEARCH Across Five Aprils

```
X T T Z C O N F E D E R A T E S N B M D
W X L J V B D N X S M H M P K V P L Q N
P B C T P S W R V R C J J B B V F Y M Q
L Q M L M Y O S H A D R A C H X N X J N
S R F Y C X R B F P C P M B E D L F F P
Q H X A M P T J Y Z B J K Z L J O C N S
X G N L M R M D E M J H O E L H C G O Z
P V T Y R E A N H N N V V H E E N C S K
R Y D O O H N A M E N A D E N B I L L C
H H M F M R N D S A D Y N O C Y L L I B
D L J N A N P L M U T J T C B Z U K W R
B E J B A S I R L E J T M S Y B N R Q C
S E S V A W U T O G N E G O B L U F F S
X H A E X P S M X S C T T R X R H R N M
C S I H R Q P R T N P V L H A Q I T O G
K H D L E T S O A E Y E K R R N X D T J
H L I B O N E D M A R Y C H S O T A G X
M Y T L P H R R I A H F C T C W P E N E
C Q C U D Q F Y L J T R G D A F G R I C
T H H D R H Z J T Z N T L R R Q B J H Z
X G E Z H K O T O Q T M O N E S M P S M
F G S C F X E O N Z M N J X D S G K A S
B L P W F M K Y D S H H X T Z G S B W T
```

ADULTS	CONFEDERATES	HENRY	MILTON	SUMTER
AMENDMENT	DAN	JENNY	NANCY	TOM
APPOMATTOX	DANCE	JETHRO	PROSPECT	TURKEY
BARN	DAVE	JOHN	READ	WASHINGTON
BILL	DESERTER	LEE	ROSCOE	WILSE
BLUFF	DITCHES	LINCOLN	SAVANNAH	WILSON
BRIDGE	EB	MANHOOD	SCARED	WORTMAN
BULL	ELLEN	MARY	SHADRACH	
CHILDHOOD	GRANT	MATT	SHILOH	

WORD SEARCH ANSWER KEY Across Five Aprils

ADULTS	CONFEDERATES	HENRY	MILTON	SUMTER
AMENDMENT	DAN	JENNY	NANCY	TOM
APPOMATTOX	DANCE	JETHRO	PROSPECT	TURKEY
BARN	DAVE	JOHN	READ	WASHINGTON
BILL	DESERTER	LEE	ROSCOE	WILSE
BLUFF	DITCHES	LINCOLN	SAVANNAH	WILSON
BRIDGE	EB	MANHOOD	SCARED	WORTMAN
BULL	ELLEN	MARY	SHADRACH	
CHILDHOOD	GRANT	MATT	SHILOH	

132

CROSSWORD Across Five Aprils

Across
2. Where Mary had been the night she was killed
5. Southern general
7. President during the Civil War
9. People set the Creighton's on fire
12. Burdow who rode with Jethro & saved him
13. They were troubled by drought, elections, slavery, secession & talk of war
16. Died on the battlefield
17. The union began to win after the fall of Fort ____ in Tennessee
18. Northern general
19. Was killed in an accident
20. Editor
22. Ellen's nephew
23. Bill & he were close brothers who had a fight
24. Confederates fired on this fort and the war started

Down
1. Ball's ____
2. Lawrence; Brings news of Tom's death
3. Jethro's mother
4. Fighters for the South
6. Jethro wrote to Lincoln about his desertion
8. John's wife
10. Ellen gave the letter to Jethro because she could not ____.
11. Jethro's father
13. The 13th ____ freed slaves
14. Sherman's gift to Lincoln
15. Place where Jethro & Dave Burdow were attacked
16. Call Eb used in the woods
21. Went to fight for the South

CROSSWORD ANSWER KEY Across Five Aprils

	1 B		2 D	A	N	C	3 E		4 C		
5 L	E	6 E		A		7 L	I	8 N	C	O	L	N
U		9 B	10 A	R	N	11 M	L	A	N		
F			E	12 D	A	V	E	N	F		
F			A		T	N	C	E			
		13 A	D	U	L	14 T	S		C	Y	D	15 B
	16 T	O	M			A		17 H	E	N	R	Y
	U		E			V			R		I
18 G	R	A	N	T	19 M	A	R	Y		A	D
	K		D		N					T	G
	E	20 E	M	I	L	T	O	N	21 B	E	E
	Y		E				A	22 W	I	L	S	E
			N		23 J	O	H	N		L	
24 S	U	M	T	E	R					L	

Across
2. Where Mary had been the night she was killed
5. Southern general
7. President during the Civil War
9. People set the Creighton's on fire
12. Burdow who rode with Jethro & saved him
13. They were troubled by drought, elections, slavery, secession & talk of war
16. Died on the battlefield
17. The union began to win after the fall of Fort ____ in Tennessee
18. Northern general
19. Was killed in an accident
20. Editor
22. Ellen's nephew
23. Bill & he were close brothers who had a fight
24. Confederates fired on this fort and the war started

Down
1. Ball's ____
2. Lawrence; Brings news of Tom's death
3. Jethro's mother
4. Fighters for the South
6. Jethro wrote to Lincoln about his desertion
8. John's wife
10. Ellen gave the letter to Jethro because she could not ____.
11. Jethro's father
13. The 13th ____ freed slaves
14. Sherman's gift to Lincoln
15. Place where Jethro & Dave Burdow were attacked
16. Call Eb used in the woods
21. Went to fight for the South

MATCHING 1 Across Five Aprils

___ 1. SCARED   A. What Eb became by leaving the army
___ 2. SHILOH   B. Fighters for the South
___ 3. BRIDGE   C. Southern general
___ 4. READ   D. Jenny went there to see Shad
___ 5. PROSPECT   E. President during the Civil War
___ 6. BLUFF   F. Ellen gave the letter to Jethro because she could not ____.
___ 7. TOM   G. Place where Jethro & Dave Burdow were attacked
___ 8. SHADRACH   H. Jethro considered the victory here to be empty like Pittsburgh landing
___ 9. AMENDMENT   I. Jake; wanted Jethro to bring him a newspaper
___10. ELLEN   J. Eb's job was digging these when he rejoined the army
___11. APPOMATTOX   K. Young boy who grew up during the Civil War
___12. HENRY   L. Point ____; deserters' camp
___13. WORTMAN   M. Bill told Jethro that being ____ was nothing to be ashamed of
___14. ROSCOE   N. Jethro's going to town alone was a step towards his ____.
___15. WILSE   O. Ball's ____
___16. LEE   P. Courthouse where the South surrendered
___17. MARY   Q. Mob leader who threatened Jethro
___18. DESERTER   R. Jethro's mother
___19. LINCOLN   S. Sherman's gift to Lincoln
___20. SAVANNAH   T. Died on the battlefield
___21. JETHRO   U. Ellen's nephew
___22. CONFEDERATES   V. Teacher
___23. MANHOOD   W. The union began to win after the fall of Fort ____ in Tennessee
___24. WASHINGTON   X. The 13th ____ freed slaves
___25. DITCHES   Y. Was killed in an accident

MATCHING 1 ANSWER KEY Across Five Aprils

M - 1. SCARED	A.	What Eb became by leaving the army
H - 2. SHILOH	B.	Fighters for the South
G - 3. BRIDGE	C.	Southern general
F - 4. READ	D.	Jenny went there to see Shad
L - 5. PROSPECT	E.	President during the Civil War
O - 6. BLUFF	F.	Ellen gave the letter to Jethro because she could not ____.
T - 7. TOM	G.	Place where Jethro & Dave Burdow were attacked
V - 8. SHADRACH	H.	Jethro considered the victory here to be empty like Pittsburgh landing
X - 9. AMENDMENT	I.	Jake; wanted Jethro to bring him a newspaper
R - 10. ELLEN	J.	Eb's job was digging these when he rejoined the army
P - 11. APPOMATTOX	K.	Young boy who grew up during the Civil War
W - 12. HENRY	L.	Point ____; deserters' camp
Q - 13. WORTMAN	M.	Bill told Jethro that being ____ was nothing to be ashamed of
I - 14. ROSCOE	N.	Jethro's going to town alone was a step towards his ____.
U - 15. WILSE	O.	Ball's ____
C - 16. LEE	P.	Courthouse where the South surrendered
Y - 17. MARY	Q.	Mob leader who threatened Jethro
A - 18. DESERTER	R.	Jethro's mother
E - 19. LINCOLN	S.	Sherman's gift to Lincoln
S - 20. SAVANNAH	T.	Died on the battlefield
K - 21. JETHRO	U.	Ellen's nephew
B - 22. CONFEDERATES	V.	Teacher
N - 23. MANHOOD	W.	The union began to win after the fall of Fort ____ in Tennessee
D - 24. WASHINGTON	X.	The 13th ____ freed slaves
J - 25. DITCHES	Y.	Was killed in an accident

MATCHING 2 Across Five Aprils

___ 1. WASHINGTON   A. Jethro's mother
___ 2. GRANT   B. Point ____; deserters' camp
___ 3. SAVANNAH   C. Jenny went there to see Shad
___ 4. TOM   D. Where Mary had been the night she was killed
___ 5. SHADRACH   E. Ellen gave the letter to Jethro because she could not ____.
___ 6. TURKEY   F. Young boy who grew up during the Civil War
___ 7. BULL   G. Courthouse where the South surrendered
___ 8. HENRY   H. Jethro's father
___ 9. ELLEN   I. Jethro wrote to Lincoln about his desertion
___10. MILTON   J. ____ Run
___11. JOHN   K. Ball's ____
___12. READ   L. Sherman's gift to Lincoln
___13. PROSPECT   M. Call Eb used in the woods
___14. CONFEDERATES   N. Lawrence; Brings news of Tom's death
___15. APPOMATTOX   O. Died on the battlefield
___16. DAN   P. Fighters for the South
___17. DANCE   Q. Teacher
___18. SHILOH   R. Editor
___19. EB   S. Jake; wanted Jethro to bring him a newspaper
___20. NANCY   T. Northern general
___21. ROSCOE   U. John's wife
___22. BLUFF   V. What Eb became by leaving the army
___23. MATT   W. Jethro considered the victory here to be empty like Pittsburgh landing
___24. JETHRO   X. Bill & he were close brothers who had a fight
___25. DESERTER   Y. The union began to win after the fall of Fort ____ in Tennessee

MATCHING 2 ANSWER KEY Across Five Aprils

C - 1. WASHINGTON	A.	Jethro's mother
T - 2. GRANT	B.	Point ____; deserters' camp
L - 3. SAVANNAH	C.	Jenny went there to see Shad
O - 4. TOM	D.	Where Mary had been the night she was killed
Q - 5. SHADRACH	E.	Ellen gave the letter to Jethro because she could not ____.
M - 6. TURKEY	F.	Young boy who grew up during the Civil War
J - 7. BULL	G.	Courthouse where the South surrendered
Y - 8. HENRY	H.	Jethro's father
A - 9. ELLEN	I.	Jethro wrote to Lincoln about his desertion
R -10. MILTON	J.	____ Run
X -11. JOHN	K.	Ball's ____
E -12. READ	L.	Sherman's gift to Lincoln
B -13. PROSPECT	M.	Call Eb used in the woods
P -14. CONFEDERATES	N.	Lawrence; Brings news of Tom's death
G -15. APPOMATTOX	O.	Died on the battlefield
N -16. DAN	P.	Fighters for the South
D -17. DANCE	Q.	Teacher
W 18. SHILOH	R.	Editor
I - 19. EB	S.	Jake; wanted Jethro to bring him a newspaper
U -20. NANCY	T.	Northern general
S -21. ROSCOE	U.	John's wife
K -22. BLUFF	V.	What Eb became by leaving the army
H -23. MATT	W.	Jethro considered the victory here to be empty like Pittsburgh landing
F -24. JETHRO	X.	Bill & he were close brothers who had a fight
V -25. DESERTER	Y.	The union began to win after the fall of Fort ____ in Tennessee

JUGGLE LETTERS Across Five Aprils

1. TMAAOTPXPO = 1. _____
Courthouse where the South surrendered

2. OSHIHL = 2. _____
Jethro considered the victory here to be empty like Pittsburgh landing

3. FFLUB = 3. _____
Ball's ____

4. ECOPRTPS = 4. _____
Point ____; deserters' camp

5. BE = 5. _____
Jethro wrote to Lincoln about his desertion

6. CRSADE = 6. _____
Bill told Jethro that being ____ was nothing to be ashamed of

7. DARCHHAS = 7. _____
Teacher

8. ROTHJE = 8. _____
Young boy who grew up during the Civil War

9. NEYNJ = 9. _____
Married Shad Yale

10. LOTMNI =10. _____
Editor

11. TC DIHSE =11. _____
Eb's job was digging these when he rejoined the army

12. OAMOHND =12. _____
Jethro's going to town alone was a step towards his ____.

13. DNA =13. _____
Lawrence; Brings news of Tom's death

14. EEL =14. _____
Southern general

15. MTO =15. _____
Died on the battlefield

16. ADRE =16. _____
Ellen gave the letter to Jethro because she could not ____.

17. CSOROE =17. _____
Jake; wanted Jethro to bring him a newspaper

18. EMETNMADN =18. _____
The 13th ____ freed slaves

19. CNILLON =19. _____
President during the Civil War

20. ILWES =20. _____
Ellen's nephew

21. HAVANSNA =21. _____
Sherman's gift to Lincoln

22. RABN =22. _____
People set the Creighton's on fire

23. TLDAUS =23. _____
They were troubled by drought, elections, slavery, secession & talk of war

24. IDHOHLCDO =24. _____
Jethro left his behind him in March 1862

25. AENSREDOCEFT =25. _____
Fighters for the South

26. ECNDA =26. _____
Where Mary had been the night she was killed

27. GERIDB =27. _____
Place where Jethro & Dave Burdow were attacked

28. RDTESREE =28. _____
What Eb became by leaving the army

29. NYNAC =29. _____
John's wife

30. NHJO =30. _____
Bill & he were close brothers who had a fight

31. ENLEL =31. _____
Jethro's mother

32. GNSIHATOWN =32. _____
Jenny went there to see Shad

33. LILB =33. _____
Went to fight for the South

34. TGNAR =34. _____
Northern general

35. LNOSWI =35. _____
____'s Creek; battle close to Creighton's home; Union lost

36. YARM =36. _____
Was killed in an accident

37. MTTA =37. _____
Jethro's father

38. AEVD =38. _____
Burdow who rode with Jethro & saved him

39. LULB =39. _____
____ Run

40. TRSEMU =40. _____
Confederates fired on this fort and the war started

41. TNMROAW =41. _____
Mob leader who threatened Jethro

42. RHEYN =42. _____
The union began to win after the fall of Fort ____ in Tennessee

43. YTRUEK =43. _____
Call Eb used in the woods

JUGGLE LETTERS ANSWER KEY Across Five Aprils

1. TMAAOTPXPO = 1. APPOMATTOX
   Courthouse where the South surrendered

2. OSHIHL = 2. SHILOH
   Jethro considered the victory here to be empty like Pittsburgh landing

3. FFLUB = 3. BLUFF
   Ball's ____

4. ECOPRTPS = 4. PROSPECT
   Point ____; deserters' camp

5. BE = 5. EB
   Jethro wrote to Lincoln about his desertion

6. CRSADE = 6. SCARED
   Bill told Jethro that being ____ was nothing to be ashamed of

7. DARCHHAS = 7. SHADRACH
   Teacher

8. ROTHJE = 8. JETHRO
   Young boy who grew up during the Civil War

9. NEYNJ = 9. JENNY
   Married Shad Yale

10. LOTMNI = 10. MILTON
    Editor

11. TC DIHSE = 11. DITCHES
    Eb's job was digging these when he rejoined the army

12. OAMOHND = 12. MANHOOD
    Jethro's going to town alone was a step towards his ____.

13. DNA = 13. DAN
    Lawrence; Brings news of Tom's death

14. EEL = 14. LEE
    Southern general

15. MTO =15. TOM
Died on the battlefield

16. ADRE =16. READ
Ellen gave the letter to Jethro because she could not ____.

17. CSOROE =17. ROSCOE
Jake; wanted Jethro to bring him a newspaper

18. EMETNMADN =18. AMENDMENT
The 13th ____ freed slaves

19. CNILLON =19. LINCOLN
President during the Civil War

20. ILWES =20. WILSE
Ellen's nephew

21. HAVANSNA =21. SAVANNAH
Sherman's gift to Lincoln

22. RABN =22. BARN
People set the Creighton's on fire

23. TLDAUS =23. ADULTS
They were troubled by drought, elections, slavery, secession & talk of war

24. IDHOHLCDO =24. CHILDHOOD
Jethro left his behind him in March 1862

25. AENSREDOCEFT =25. CONFEDERATES
Fighters for the South

26. ECNDA =26. DANCE
Where Mary had been the night she was killed

27. GERIDB =27. BRIDGE
Place where Jethro & Dave Burdow were attacked

28. RDTESREE =28. DESERTER
What Eb became by leaving the army

29. NYNAC =29. NANCY
John's wife

30. NHJO =30. JOHN
Bill & he were close brothers who had a fight

31. ENLEL =31. ELLEN
Jethro's mother

32. GNSIHATOWN =32. WASHINGTON
Jenny went there to see Shad

33. LILB =33. BILL
Went to fight for the South

34. TGNAR =34. GRANT
Northern general

35. LNOSWI =35. WILSON
____'s Creek; battle close to Creighton's home; Union lost

36. YARM =36. MARY
Was killed in an accident

37. MTTA =37. MATT
Jethro's father

38. AEVD =38. DAVE
Burdow who rode with Jethro & saved him

39. LULB =39. BULL
____ Run

40. TRSEMU =40. SUMTER
Confederates fired on this fort and the war started

41. TNMROAW =41. WORTMAN
Mob leader who threatened Jethro

42. RHEYN =42. HENRY
The union began to win after the fall of Fort ____ in Tennessee

43. YTRUEK =43. TURKEY
Call Eb used in the woods

VOCABULARY RESOURCE MATERIALS

Across Five Aprils Vocabulary Word List

No.	Word	Clue/Definition
1.	ABOLITIONISTS	People who wanted no more slavery
2.	ADMONITIONS	Reprimands
3.	AGONIZINGLY	With great pain or difficult
4.	ALLUSION	Indirect reference
5.	AMENDED	Fixed; corrected
6.	AMIABLE	Good-natured; friendly
7.	ANNEX	An addition or auxiliary building
8.	APATHY	Indifference
9.	ASTUTE	Shrewd; smart concerning one's own affairs
10.	BELLIGERENTLY	Defiantly; in a hostile manner
11.	BROOKED	Tolerated
12.	BUNTING	Strips of material in patriotic colors used for festive decorations
13.	CAUSTICALLY	Capable of burning; in a fiery manner
14.	COMPATRIOTS	People from one's own country or team
15.	CONTAGION	A bad influence; the spreading of an idea
16.	CONTEMPTUOUS	Scornful
17.	CREDENCE	Believability
18.	CULPRITS	People charged with crimes
19.	DEFILED	Polluted
20.	DESPERADO	Desperate outlaw
21.	DISSIPATED	Dispersed; sent or went away
22.	ENDURANCE	Strength over a long period of time
23.	FATIGUE	Being physically or emotionally tired
24.	GAIETY	Festivity; happiness
25.	GANGRENOUS	Having decaying bodily tissues
26.	GENIALLY	Kindly; pleasantly
27.	HARBOR	To shelter
28.	IMMINENCE	The quality of being about to happen
29.	INCOHERENT	Disjointed; not in an orderly manner
30.	INEPT	Incompetent
31.	IRONCLADS	19th century was ships having sides with metal plates as armor
32.	LOATHING	Feeling of repulsion
33.	MAMMOTH	Huge
34.	OMINOUS	Threatening
35.	PANDEMONIUM	Wild uproar
36.	PASSEL	A bunch; many
37.	PERMEATING	Penetrating; spreading throughout
38.	PREOCCUPATION	Something that engrosses the mind
39.	PREPONDERANCE	Majority
40.	PROVENDER	Food for animals
41.	QUAGMIRE	Soft, muddy land
42.	REITERATED	Said or did something repeatedly
43.	REVERBERATION	An echo-like effect
44.	SHUNNED	Deliberately avoided
45.	STARK	Bare; harsh; desolate
46.	TACIT	Unspoken
47.	TENACITY	Holding or sticking to something persistently
48.	TETHERED	Tied with a short rope or string
49.	TUMULT	Agitation of the mind or emotions; a disturbance
50.	TYRANNICAL	Oppressively domineering

Across Five Aprils Vocabulary Word List Continued

No.	Word	Clue/Definition
51.	VINDICTIVENESS	Revengefulness
52.	WANLY	In a way showing one tired or sad
53.	WASTREL	One who wastes things

VOCABULARY WORD SEARCH Across Five Aprils

ABOLITIONISTS	CAUSTICALLY	GANGRENOUS	PERMEATING
ADMONITIONS	COMPATRIOTS	GENIALLY	PREPONDERANCE
AGONIZINGLY	CONTAGION	HARBOR	PROVENDER
ALLUSION	CONTEMPTUOUS	IMMINENCE	QUAGMIRE
AMENDED	CREDENCE	INCOHERENT	SHUNNED
AMIABLE	CULPRITS	INEPT	STARK
ANNEX	DEFILED	IRONCLADS	TACIT
APATHY	DESPERADO	LOATHING	TENACITY
ASTUTE	DISSIPATED	MAMMOTH	TETHERED
BELLIGERENTLY	ENDURANCE	OMINOUS	TUMULT
BROOKED	FATIGUE	PANDEMONIUM	WANLY
BUNTING	GAIETY	PASSEL	WASTREL

VOCABULARY WORD SEARCH ANSWER KEY Across Five Aprils

```
T D T S   L B U N T I N G S S   M   M A Y
E I A D M O N I T I O N S T U M U L T E
N S C A   A   N     U T A O A I L I
A S I L M T   E     O W R N M N U A
C I T C   H   R     O A K I M S G
I P E N   I   R H   C N C M O I O
T A T E   N R G L E U L T O P N N
Y T H P T G E B C D L P A M E A I
L E R I   N A S R N I M T P R B Z
T E E A   S A W I T A O E R O I
N D D T U H     A C S M P O M L N
E N P     S P E   I N T I G
R E     U B E A T E U E T L
E M E   N T R D G D A I I Y
G A N N E X R O H R T N O F
I   A   E I E D   U A G D N A
L     D M U O K Y S N E I T
L     G R A M I A B L E C R S I
E B         I M M I N E N C E L T G
  Q N O I G A T N O C     E   S U
          O D A R E P S E D     E
          C A U S T I C A L L Y
```

ABOLITIONISTS	CAUSTICALLY	GANGRENOUS	PERMEATING
ADMONITIONS	COMPATRIOTS	GENIALLY	PREPONDERANCE
AGONIZINGLY	CONTAGION	HARBOR	PROVENDER
ALLUSION	CONTEMPTUOUS	IMMINENCE	QUAGMIRE
AMENDED	CREDENCE	INCOHERENT	SHUNNED
AMIABLE	CULPRITS	INEPT	STARK
ANNEX	DEFILED	IRONCLADS	TACIT
APATHY	DESPERADO	LOATHING	TENACITY
ASTUTE	DISSIPATED	MAMMOTH	TETHERED
BELLIGERENTLY	ENDURANCE	OMINOUS	TUMULT
BROOKED	FATIGUE	PANDEMONIUM	WANLY
BUNTING	GAIETY	PASSEL	WASTREL

VOCABULARY CROSSWORD Across Five Apils

Across
1. With great pain or difficult
6. Polluted
8. Unspoken
10. Reprimands
12. One who wastes things
13. Bare; harsh; desolate
14. Fixed; corrected
15. Good-natured; friendly
16. In a way showing one tired or sad
17. People who wanted no more slavery

Down
1. Indirect reference
2. Incompetent
3. The quality of being about to happen
4. Festivity; happiness
5. Indifference
7. Dispersed; sent or went away
9. Capable of burning; in a fiery manner
11. Desperate outlaw

VOCABULARY CROSSWORD ANSWER KEY Across Five Aprils

			1 A	G	2 O	N	3 I	Z	4 I	N	G	L	Y	
			L			N		M		A				5 A
6 D	E	F	I	L	E	D	7 D		E		M		I		P
			U			I		P		I		E		A
			S			S		T		I		8 T	A	9 C	I	T
			I			S				E		Y		A		H
	10 A	11 D	M	O	N	I	T	I	O	N	S			U		Y
		E		N			P			C				S		
		S			12 W	A	S	T	R	E	L		13 S	T	A	R	K
		P			A		T						I		
		E		14 A	M	E	N	D	E	D			C		
		R			D						15 A	M	I	A	B	L	E
	16 W	A	N	L	Y								L		
		D											L		
17 A	B	O	L	I	T	I	O	N	I	S	T	S		Y		

Across
1. With great pain or difficult
6. Polluted
8. Unspoken
10. Reprimands
12. One who wastes things
13. Bare; harsh; desolate
14. Fixed; corrected
15. Good-natured; friendly
16. In a way showing one tired or sad
17. People who wanted no more slavery

Down
1. Indirect reference
2. Incompetent
3. The quality of being about to happen
4. Festivity; happiness
5. Indifference
7. Dispersed; sent or went away
9. Capable of burning; in a fiery manner
11. Desperate outlaw

VOCABULARY MATCHING 1 Across Five Aprils

___ 1. DESPERADO   A. Bare; harsh; desolate

___ 2. BROOKED   B. One who wastes things

___ 3. APATHY   C. Defiantly; in a hostile manner

___ 4. ANNEX   D. Holding or sticking to something persistently

___ 5. DISSIPATED   E. Good-natured; friendly

___ 6. BUNTING   F. Majority

___ 7. INEPT   G. A bunch; many

___ 8. GANGRENOUS   H. Wild uproar

___ 9. IMMINENCE   I. Reprimands

___10. CAUSTICALLY   J. Capable of burning; in a fiery manner

___11. GAIETY   K. Indifference

___12. STARK   L. Penetrating; spreading throughout

___13. PASSEL   M. Disjointed; not in an orderly manner

___14. WASTREL   N. Festivity; happiness

___15. REITERATED   O. Food for animals

___16. TENACITY   P. Tolerated

___17. ASTUTE   Q. An addition or auxiliary building

___18. PREPONDERANCE   R. Shrewd; smart concerning one's own affairs

___19. PANDEMONIUM   S. Incompetent

___20. ADMONITIONS   T. Said or did something repeatedly

___21. PROVENDER   U. Strips of material in patriotic colors used for festive decorations

___22. PERMEATING   V. Desperate outlaw

___23. AMIABLE   W. The quality of being about to happen

___24. BELLIGERENTLY   X. Dispersed; sent or went away

___25. INCOHERENT   Y. Having decaying bodily tissues

VOCABULARY MATCHING 1 ANSWER KEY Across Five Aprils

V - 1.	DESPERADO	A. Bare; harsh; desolate
P - 2.	BROOKED	B. One who wastes things
K - 3.	APATHY	C. Defiantly; in a hostile manner
Q - 4.	ANNEX	D. Holding or sticking to something persistently
X - 5.	DISSIPATED	E. Good-natured; friendly
U - 6.	BUNTING	F. Majority
S - 7.	INEPT	G. A bunch; many
Y - 8.	GANGRENOUS	H. Wild uproar
W - 9.	IMMINENCE	I. Reprimands
J - 10.	CAUSTICALLY	J. Capable of burning; in a fiery manner
N - 11.	GAIETY	K. Indifference
A - 12.	STARK	L. Penetrating; spreading throughout
G - 13.	PASSEL	M. Disjointed; not in an orderly manner
B - 14.	WASTREL	N. Festivity; happiness
T - 15.	REITERATED	O. Food for animals
D - 16.	TENACITY	P. Tolerated
R - 17.	ASTUTE	Q. An addition or auxiliary building
F - 18.	PREPONDERANCE	R. Shrewd; smart concerning one's own affairs
H - 19.	PANDEMONIUM	S. Incompetent
I - 20.	ADMONITIONS	T. Said or did something repeatedly
O - 21.	PROVENDER	U. Strips of material in patriotic colors used for festive decorations
L - 22.	PERMEATING	V. Desperate outlaw
E - 23.	AMIABLE	W. The quality of being about to happen
C - 24.	BELLIGERENTLY	X. Dispersed; sent or went away
M - 25.	INCOHERENT	Y. Having decaying bodily tissues

VOCABULARY MATCHING 2 Across Five Aprils

___ 1. AGONIZINGLY   A. Something that engrosses the mind
___ 2. ALLUSION   B. Disjointed; not in an orderly manner
___ 3. CAUSTICALLY   C. Feeling of repulsion
___ 4. ENDURANCE   D. Penetrating; spreading throughout
___ 5. CREDENCE   E. An echo-like effect
___ 6. BELLIGERENTLY   F. With great pain or difficult
___ 7. REVERBERATION   G. Having decaying bodily tissues
___ 8. STARK   H. Revengefulness
___ 9. TUMULT   I. Desperate outlaw
___ 10. VINDICTIVENESS   J. Indifference
___ 11. ASTUTE   K. Believability
___ 12. DISSIPATED   L. Agitation of the mind or emotions; a disturbance
___ 13. APATHY   M. Strips of material in patriotic colors used for festive decorations
___ 14. LOATHING   N. Dispersed; sent or went away
___ 15. CONTEMPTUOUS   O. Strength over a long period of time
___ 16. TYRANNICAL   P. Defiantly; in a hostile manner
___ 17. GANGRENOUS   Q. Oppressively domineering
___ 18. COMPATRIOTS   R. People from one's own country or team
___ 19. WANLY   S. A bunch; many
___ 20. BUNTING   T. In a way showing one tired or sad
___ 21. PERMEATING   U. Scornful
___ 22. PASSEL   V. Capable of burning; in a fiery manner
___ 23. DESPERADO   W. Bare; harsh; desolate
___ 24. INCOHERENT   X. Shrewd; smart concerning one's own affairs
___ 25. PREOCCUPATION   Y. Indirect reference

VOCABULARY MATCHING 2 ANSWER KEY Across Five Aprils

F - 1.	AGONIZINGLY	A. Something that engrosses the mind
Y - 2.	ALLUSION	B. Disjointed; not in an orderly manner
V - 3.	CAUSTICALLY	C. Feeling of repulsion
O - 4.	ENDURANCE	D. Penetrating; spreading throughout
K - 5.	CREDENCE	E. An echo-like effect
P - 6.	BELLIGERENTLY	F. With great pain or difficult
E - 7.	REVERBERATION	G. Having decaying bodily tissues
W 8.	STARK	H. Revengefulness
L - 9.	TUMULT	I. Desperate outlaw
H -10.	VINDICTIVENESS	J. Indifference
X -11.	ASTUTE	K. Believability
N -12.	DISSIPATED	L. Agitation of the mind or emotions; a disturbance
J - 13.	APATHY	M. Strips of material in patriotic colors used for festive decorations
C -14.	LOATHING	N. Dispersed; sent or went away
U -15.	CONTEMPTUOUS	O. Strength over a long period of time
Q -16.	TYRANNICAL	P. Defiantly; in a hostile manner
G -17.	GANGRENOUS	Q. Oppressively domineering
R -18.	COMPATRIOTS	R. People from one's own country or team
T -19.	WANLY	S. A bunch; many
M 20.	BUNTING	T. In a way showing one tired or sad
D -21.	PERMEATING	U. Scornful
S -22.	PASSEL	V. Capable of burning; in a fiery manner
I - 23.	DESPERADO	W. Bare; harsh; desolate
B -24.	INCOHERENT	X. Shrewd; smart concerning one's own affairs
A -25.	PREOCCUPATION	Y. Indirect reference

VOCABULARY JUGGLE LETTERS Across Five Aprils

1. NCDENRPAREOEP = 1. _____
   Majority

2. UADPNENMMOI = 2. _____
   Wild uproar

3. ADPTISEIDS = 3. _____
   Dispersed; sent or went away

4. OEBDKOR = 4. _____
   Tolerated

5. NCRAYITNLA = 5. _____
   Oppressively domineering

6. EENYIBETGRLLL = 6. _____
   Defiantly; in a hostile manner

7. NHENUDS = 7. _____
   Deliberately avoided

8. DNRENCAUE = 8. _____
   Strength over a long period of time

9. TTCAI = 9. _____
   Unspoken

10. BITOOSTSINIAL =10. _____
    People who wanted no more slavery

11. TAGYEI =11. _____
    Festivity; happiness

12. EAUTTS =12. _____
    Shrewd; smart concerning one's own affairs

13. NCERDECE =13. _____
    Believability

14. NSDOICLRA =14. _____
    19th century was ships having sides with metal plates as armor

15. AMTMOMH =15. _____
Huge

16. NEIECMMIN =16. _____
The quality of being about to happen

17. UNTINGB =17. _____
Strips of material in patriotic colors used for festive decorations

18. NTSNDIOMAIO =18. _____
Reprimands

19. ATLWRSE =19. _____
One who wastes things

20. ETNAOEVBIRRER =20. _____
An echo-like effect

21. SREAUNONGG =21. _____
Having decaying bodily tissues

22. NIONHEERCT =22. _____
Disjointed; not in an orderly manner

23. OAERDESPD =23. _____
Desperate outlaw

24. FDDIEEL =24. _____
Polluted

25. NLAEILYG =25. _____
Kindly; pleasantly

26. ETRAEREDTI =26. _____
Said or did something repeatedly

27. HAPATY =27. _____
Indifference

28. TAGUIFE =28. _____
Being physically or emotionally tired

29. MILEBAA =29. _____
Good-natured; friendly

30. IYEATNCT =30. _____
Holding or sticking to something persistently

31. DADMEEN =31. _____
Fixed; corrected

32. ZINAGNYOLGI =32. _____
With great pain or difficult

33. HEETEDRT =33. _____
Tied with a short rope or string

34. MIOSOUN =34. _____
Threatening

35. ITEMRAGEPN =35. _____
Penetrating; spreading throughout

36. LNSLOIUA =36. _____
Indirect reference

37. NXNAE =37. _____
An addition or auxiliary building

38. TUUMTL =38. _____
Agitation of the mind or emotions; a disturbance

39. NPTEI =39. _____
Incompetent

40. SDECINVNVISETI =40. _____
Revengefulness

41. SEPSLA =41. _____
A bunch; many

42. RDRNPOEEV =42. _____
Food for animals

43. HTONGAIL =43. _____
Feeling of repulsion

44. EAQMIGRU =44. _____
Soft, muddy land

45. ONTINOAGC =45. _____
A bad influence; the spreading of an idea

46. KASRT =46. _____
Bare; harsh; desolate

47. CUPEONITOARPC =47. _____
Something that engrosses the mind

48. LAWNY =48. _____
In a way showing one tired or sad

49. TOTONSUEUCPM =49. _____
Scornful

50. ILSACTLAYUC =50. _____
Capable of burning; in a fiery manner

VOCABULARY JUGGLE LETTERS ANSWER KEY Across Five Aprils

1. NCDENRPAREOEP = 1. PREPONDERANCE
Majority

2. UADPNENMMOI = 2. PANDEMONIUM
Wild uproar

3. ADPTISEIDS = 3. DISSIPATED
Dispersed; sent or went away

4. OEBDKOR = 4. BROOKED
Tolerated

5. NCRAYITNLA = 5. TYRANNICAL
Oppressively domineering

6. EENYIBETGRLLL = 6. BELLIGERENTLY
Defiantly; in a hostile manner

7. NHENUDS = 7. SHUNNED
Deliberately avoided

8. DNRENCAUE = 8. ENDURANCE
Strength over a long period of time

9. TTCAI = 9. TACIT
Unspoken

10. BITOOSTSINIAL =10. ABOLITIONISTS
People who wanted no more slavery

11. TAGYEI =11. GAIETY
Festivity; happiness

12. EAUTTS =12. ASTUTE
Shrewd; smart concerning one's own affairs

13. NCERDECE =13. CREDENCE
Believability

14. NSDOICLRA =14. IRONCLADS
19th century was ships having sides with metal plates as armor

15. AMTMOMH =15. MAMMOTH
Huge

16. NEIECMMIN =16. IMMINENCE
The quality of being about to happen

17. UNTINGB =17. BUNTING
Strips of material in patriotic colors used for festive decorations

18. NTSNDIOMAIO =18. ADMONITIONS
Reprimands

19. ATLWRSE =19. WASTREL
One who wastes things

20. ETNAOEVBIRRER =20. REVERBERATION
An echo-like effect

21. SREAUNONGG =21. GANGRENOUS
Having decaying bodily tissues

22. NIONHEERCT =22. INCOHERENT
Disjointed; not in an orderly manner

23. OAERDESPD =23. DESPERADO
Desperate outlaw

24. FDDIEEL =24. DEFILED
Polluted

25. NLAEILYG =25. GENIALLY
Kindly; pleasantly

26. ETRAEREDTI =26. REITERATED
Said or did something repeatedly

27. HAPATY =27. APATHY
Indifference

28. TAGUIFE =28. FATIGUE
Being physically or emotionally tired

29. MILEBAA =29. AMIABLE
Good-natured; friendly

30. IYEATNCT =30. TENACITY
Holding or sticking to something persistently

31. DADMEEN	=31.	AMENDED
		Fixed; corrected
32. ZINAGNYOLGI	=32.	AGONIZINGLY
		With great pain or difficult
33. HEETEDRT	=33.	TETHERED
		Tied with a short rope or string
34. MIOSOUN	=34.	OMINOUS
		Threatening
35. ITEMRAGEPN	=35.	PERMEATING
		Penetrating; spreading throughout
36. LNSLOIUA	=36.	ALLUSION
		Indirect reference
37. NXNAE	=37.	ANNEX
		An addition or auxiliary building
38. TUUMTL	=38.	TUMULT
		Agitation of the mind or emotions; a disturbance
39. NPTEI	=39.	INEPT
		Incompetent
40. SDECINVNVISETI	=40.	VINDICTIVENESS
		Revengefulness
41. SEPSLA	=41.	PASSEL
		A bunch; many
42. RDRNPOEEV	=42.	PROVENDER
		Food for animals
43. HTONGAIL	=43.	LOATHING
		Feeling of repulsion
44. EAQMIGRU	=44.	QUAGMIRE
		Soft, muddy land
45. ONTINOAGC	=45.	CONTAGION
		A bad influence; the spreading of an idea
46. KASRT	=46.	STARK
		Bare; harsh; desolate

47. CUPEONITOARPC =47. PREOCCUPATION
Something that engrosses the mind

48. LAWNY =48. WANLY
In a way showing one tired or sad

49. TOTONSUEUCPM =49. CONTEMPTUOUS
Scornful

50. ILSACTLAYUC =50. CAUSTICALLY
Capable of burning; in a fiery manner

www.ingramcontent.com/pod-product-compliance
Lightning Source LLC
Chambersburg PA
CBHW051409070526
44584CB00023B/3352